C17/12

UNFINISHED

UNFINISHED

George Appleton

remembers and reflects

COLLINS
8 Grafton Street, London W1X 3LA

William Collins Sons & Co. Ltd
London · Glasgow · Sydney · Auckland
Toronto · Johannesburg

First published in Great Britain in 1990 by
Collins Religious Division,
part of the Collins Publishing Group
8 Grafton Street, London W1X 3LA

Printed in Great Britain at the
University Press, Cambridge

Contents

Illustrations

The cricket team at St Augustine's Missionary College, Canterbury,
   c.1925. George is seated on the right of the front row
George and Marjorie on their wedding day in Rangoon Cathedral,
   1929
Marjorie with her two daughters, Rachel and Margaret
Students and staff of St Mary's Teacher Training School,
   Kemmendine, c.1935
George with General Aung San addressing Public Relations Officers
   in Rangoon in the late 1940s
The War Memorial Reredos at St George's, Headstone, Harrow, 1948
Margaret, Timothy, George, Marjorie and Rachel on the vicarage
   lawn in Harrow, 1950
On arrival in Perth, Western Australia, 1963
With a representative of the Australian Aborigine community
The Archbishop licenses Deaconesses to baptise, preach and take part
   in divine worship, 1967
As interpreter between a Burmese monk and Archbishop Michael
   Ramsey
In Rome with Pope Paul VI, 1968
The new Archbishop in Jerusalem being received by the President of
   Israel, 1969
With Archbishop Makarios (centre) in Cyprus, 1969
Greeting the Armenian patriarch, Yegishe Derderian, 1969
In Beirut, meeting Arab Christians from the Near East Christian
   Council
With Mayor Teddy Kollek in Jerusalem
George in his early sixties while Archbishop of Perth, Australia

Great is the power of memory, exceeding great:
. . . Men go forth to wonder at the height of mountains,
at huge waves of the sea, the broad flow of rivers,
the extent of the ocean, the courses of the stars . . .
and forget to wonder at themselves.

St Augustine, *Confessions* X, 15.

Acknowledgements

The author and publishers gratefully acknowledge permission to reproduce the following copyright material:

Eric Milner-White: Prayers from *My God, My Glory* and *A Procession of Passion Prayers* reprinted by permission of SPCK, London. *My God, My Glory* is the copyright of the Friends of York Minster, 1954, 1967.

Jan Struther: Prayers from *Enlarged Songs of Praise* reprinted by permission of Oxford University Press.

Introduction

Ever since I retired from Jerusalem in 1974, friends and publishers have pressed me to write an account of what they describe as an interesting and adventurous life. From time to time I have spasmodically tried to do this, but pastoral considerations and the needs of trusting people who have come to me in the hope of getting some light on their personal problems have taken priority. Now that that pressure has lessened, and the limitations of old age have become more apparent, with also the realisation that the time of my migration into the spiritual and eternal order is drawing near, I am accepting the priority while I have time and facility for thought and expression.

I have tried to avoid a chronicle of one event after another, and now that something has been written, to examine it critically, as if cross-examining my motives, and regretting what now appears to be immaturity, self-seeking or excusing. To put it in other words, I am now the accused and the accuser. Anyone who makes a practice of standing in the presence of God most Holy, cannot fail to be aware of how far he falls short of Christ's standards of goodness, to say nothing of falling short of God's grace and glory.

The conviction that has become increasingly clear in the closing stage of a long life is that God's creation of me was not finished with my physical birth. I am still unfinished and the completion will need more than this life. In a similar way I have learnt that God's creation of the world and his perfecting of human society is still going on and may take as long in the future as it has been going on in the past. For every new generation seems to "start from scratch" and needs to be liberated from its failures,

1

recalcitrance and blatant or secret self-seeking. To encourage us there is the gospel of forgiveness, and we have reason to believe that it will exceed the seventy times seven which God asks of our own forgiveness of others for the harm done to us, either real or imagined.

The title *Unfinished* has another facet, in that it implies a belief that there is life beyond this human spell of seventy years and the increasing strain of the next ten years or more. I am deeply grateful for the firm faith of the writer of the book of Wisdom, one of the books of the Apocrypha, which we Christians might speak of as the Middle Testament:

> For Thou lovest all the things that are,
>   and abhorrest nothing which Thou hast made;
> for never wouldest Thou have made any thing
>   if Thou hadst hated it.
> And how could any thing have endured,
>   if it had not been Thy will?
> But Thou sparest all: for they are Thine,
>   O Lord, Thou lover of souls.
>
> Wisdom 11:24-6

I have much more to be thankful for, and if I were to call from memory the many people who have encouraged and befriended me, the list would occupy several pages of small telephone directory names.

The writer of the book of Ecclesiastes in the First Testament says, "Of making many books there is no end; and much study is a weariness of the flesh." I am grateful to the many books I have read, for the inspiration and insights I have received from the writers, and in a very full and busy life I have gratefully welcomed opportunities for quiet study.

In addition to all the enjoyment of life, there is the expectance and assurance of reunion with loved ones who have already crossed over the frontier between this world and the next. I dare to hope that in the providence of God they are permitted to know something of how we are faring and may know the time of our crossing and be at the arrival point to welcome us and tell us something of the joy and glory ahead.

G.A.
Epiphany 1990

CHAPTER 1

In My Beginning

I was born in 1902 in Windsor, where my father was head gardener on a small estate named Abbey House, and where my mother had been cook. The daily contact between a young gardener and a young cook, conferring about the fruit and vegetables needed for their employer's meals, led to their falling in love and marriage, and my birth nine months later. My father came from a peasant family in Berkshire, consisting of three sons and five daughters, all of whom entered some kind of domestic service, the women rising to responsible posts as head housemaids, housekeepers and parlourmaids. I remember very little of the four years spent in Windsor except the arrival of a small suit sent by one of the powerful aunts for my fourth birthday.

My mother was left an orphan as a small girl, and adopted by an uncle who worked in the library of Eton College. He had two daughters, a little older than my mother, both of whom attended a secondary school. Lily, my mother, was not allowed to receive this additional education and from her early teens had to work as a very junior housemaid, at the beck and call of older staff.

Paul's description of the first Gentile Christians scattered round the Mediterranean coastlands of the first century AD would be true of the family into which I was born: "not many wise as men reckon wisdom, not many in positions of power or from noblest families, not many wealthy" (1 Corinthians 1:26). My parents were from a long line of good people with a strong sense of duty, living at peace with their neighbours, quick to be helpful when it was in their power, understandably a little feudal in their outlook, with a cautious eye on the squire for whom they worked, liking a glass of beer or homemade parsnip wine, and not above a bit of rabbit poaching. My father was a gardener who never earned more than two pounds a week, but we always had good vegetables. His two passions were roses (he often exhibited on behalf of his employer at the Windsor Rose Show) and his onion bed. I can see him now, treading down the soil, making shallow drills and sprinkling the seed, and watching anxiously several weeks later to see if they had germinated.

My mother was a cook who could make the most of three-pennyworth of meat pieces to enrich my father's vegetables. I can't ever remember being more than healthily hungry, nor can I ever remember coming home from school or play when my mother was not there to welcome us. My father was a gentle person, wanting peace at any price. My mother was more restless and ambitious, wanting for her children the education she had been denied. Shortly after my fourth birthday we moved to a village in Somerset with my father's employer, a retired lawyer, a bachelor, whose household was presided over by a sister-in-law whose husband had died at about the time of my birth.

Our new home at Marston Magna, a village about five miles from Yeovil and Sherborne, was a rather dilapidated old manor house, attached to Marston Court where the squire lived. I was enrolled at once in the village school which had two teachers who were sisters, one taking all the younger classes and the other the older children. We were given a thorough training in reading and spelling, in writing and arithmetic, with a weekly lesson in history, geography, nature study and drawing. When we moved some six years later to a small town again, in Berkshire, I found I was more competent in the three Rs than any other school child of my own age.

Village life at that period has been beautifully described in Flora Thompson's *Lark Rise to Candleford*. We seldom saw a motor car and any journey of more than two or three miles was accomplished by horse or pony cart. On May Day each year, we school children were taken round the houses, carrying posies of spring flowers, to sing songs of spring. Similarly the choir boys went round singing carols in the week after Christmas, being

6

regaled with refreshment at most houses, and afterwards dividing the small sums given by those who allowed us to sing. At the age of seven I joined the village church choir and from that time on the parish church was the main context of my life. My family were too poor ever to have a holiday together, and my first glimpse of the sea was on a choir outing shortly after my joining. We went by excursion train to Weymouth; I took with me from my parents twopence to spend; on the journey the vicar distributed small sums calculated on services and practices attended. From that source I received fivepence. A kind choirman gave me a threepenny bit, so my total spending money for the day amounted to tenpence. Most of this was spent on a cup and saucer for my brother Stanley Basil, two years younger, the cup bearing the inscription "A Present from Weymouth".

Our home was on the village green, less than fifty yards from the church, and across the main road through the village lay the vicarage. The vicar had two sons much about the same age as my brother and myself, so we were often invited into the vicarage to play.

The schoolmistress did not live in the School House, which was occupied by an old grannie, who every day called me to come and talk to her when she was out in her small garden, or in the cottage when the weather was less promising. She was taken ill suddenly and died. Her daughter invited me into the house, as one of her mother's friends, to see the body. That was my first touch with death. She looked very peaceful, and I was quite unafraid, interested to know what had happened. Living next door to the churchyard, I was also interested in the occasional work of the gravedigger, and after school hours would help him with the digging or the filling in of a grave, again without any sadness and certainly no feeling of fear.

One of the most frequently recurring memories of childhood is of picking primroses. Every year after the three-hours service on Good Friday, in which we choir boys were divided into three groups to lead the singing of the hymns, each group for an hour, a number of villagers went off to look for primroses in the

7

hedgerows and woods. We would pick baskets of these, which would be taken home and bunched, and on the next morning taken to church to line the choir stalls and to be put in jam jars and attached to the outside of the pews down the two aisles. Not only were we children interested in primroses but in other small flowers of spring such as violets, cowslips and later daisies, buttercups, bluebells and honeysuckle. Somehow it was the small flowers that attracted my imagination. My parents were too poor to be able to give one another a birthday present each year, though there was always a present for each of us *four* children, Stanley, Laura, Edith and myself. However, on mother's birthday which fell on 24th May, father would always bring home for her a bunch of lilies of the valley.

Next to church and school came the relationship of our family to the squire for whom my father worked. My parents lived in constant awareness of the big house and its occupants, and we children were imbued with the problem of what the squire and his household would think of any action or behaviour. I remember a recurring nightmare that has only become clear in recent years through an interest in dreams. In the nightmare my father, the under-gardener, my brother and I were throwing sticks to bring down walnuts from the great tree halfway between our home and the Court. Suddenly in the dream the great tree began to fall, and we were all running in terror to escape its fall. Looking back I can see that the fall of the tree and the resulting fear were symbolising my anxiety lest the squire should come and catch us raiding his walnut tree.

On the green outside our house my father, as the chief gardener of the village, organised the bonfire for Guy Fawkes night. All the village children had coloured flare matches, and small squibs, while all the more well-to-do people supplied rockets, Catherine wheels, and the bigger fireworks. Every autumn my mother would make a football out of old rags and we had some rare games, often getting literally bogged down after any rain, with the imitation football getting too heavy to kick any distance.

Once or twice a year there would be a village concert in the schoolroom, with recitations and songs by villagers. My mother used to sing at these. She had a lovely sweet voice, and always had to sing without piano accompaniment, for she alone knew the songs. I remember two of them by heart after over eighty years. Her favourite, and the one the villagers liked best, ran like this:

> If I should plant a tiny seed of love
> In the garden of your heart,
> Would it grow to be a great big love some day
> Or would it die and fade away?
> Would you care for it and tend it every day
> 'Till the time when all must part,
> If I should plant a tiny seed of love
> In the garden of your heart?

The second song was rather a sad one with the refrain of a forsaken lover or a widower:

> It was only a beautiful picture
> In a beautiful golden frame.

Just before my tenth birthday the squire moved up to Maidenhead, taking his whole staff with him. Here my brother and I were immediately enrolled in the choir of St Luke's church. At that time we choir boys sang the whole of Evensong every night of the week. I remember in my early months, often being cornered by the other choir boys after service or practice and being asked to say the collect for the week, which we always had to learn for Sunday school. In my simplicity I duly said the collect, which was listened to with silent interest until the end, when there would be a great burst of laughter, which mystified me. It was only much later that I realised the reason for the request and also for the resulting laughter, namely the enjoyment of a broad Somerset accent which had come with me, and traces of which can still be recognised by West Country people nearly seventy years later.

9

Training in the choir gave me a fine knowledge of the Psalms, though I must say that none of us choir boys looked forward to the fifteenth evening of the month when the set psalm had no less than seventy-three verses. We were expected to follow the lessons in our Bibles, with the result that I knew my way about the Bible very competently. Learning the collect each week was interesting; for I found that some of them were short and easy to remember, others were longer and somewhat involved in thought and language. It was only years later that I came to learn that the easily remembered collects were those that had been translated by Archbishop Cranmer from the Sacramentaries of Popes Leo, Gregory and Gelasius, while the difficult ones to remember were in almost every case the work of reformers in the sixteenth and seventeenth centuries.

The parish church helped us in other ways. At morning Sunday school every week there was a clothing club into which each child was allowed to pay threepence a week and at the end of forty-eight weeks was issued with a voucher for fourteen shillings, a very high rate of interest in those days. The voucher was then taken to a clothing or boot shop where goods were supplied to that value, often with another shilling discount. Four of my family contributed regularly, and each of us received something new just before Christmas. In the National school attached to the church a 'penny bank' was organised every Monday, generous interest being given again, and withdrawals allowed at a week's notice. I think it would be true to say that my two brothers and sister and I were products of the Anglican parochial system, at a time when almost all charitable work was carried on by the churches.

At the age of eleven I became an errand boy for a working tailor, and every Saturday, and perhaps on an evening in the week, delivered the suits and costumes that he had made, though often the finished article was well behind the promised date, so the errand boy received critical comments rather than a small tip. Before long I was promoted to sewing seams, and woe betide me if a stitch showed on the face of the cloth. One shilling on Saturday and threepence for an evening were welcome additions to the family income.

Nearing my twelfth birthday, I was fortunate enough to secure a free place at the local secondary school. This achievement stretched the small family income to purchase a school cap and satchel, and pay the school book bill every term. With the threat of war approaching, a Cadet Corps was formed and my Sunday school teacher provided the fifteen shillings necessary for the purchase of a second-hand uniform, which had to be cut down to boy's size. The annual camp for secondary schools Cadet Corps gave me my first holiday away from home, but I was so homesick that a fortnight seemed an impossibly long time before I could get back to my parents and family. For a time we small cadets guarded railway bridges, with empty carbines, but were more frightened of the dark than of possible German invaders. After two years I won an Intermediate County Scholarship which brought fifteen pounds a year in addition to free education. The termly payment from this scholarship was an evening of joy in the family, and when at sixteen the scholarship money was increased to twenty pounds per annum, it was enough to avert the danger of becoming a clerk on the Great Western Railway, a temptation which my struggling parents generously resisted. I can never be grateful enough to them for the sacrifice they made to keep me at school, when even ten shillings a week would have relieved the pressure on the food bill.

My father enlisted during the Kitchener army recruiting campaign, and life became even harder for my mother. We were allowed to live rent free in the gardener's cottage, but the family allowance from the army was less than my father had been earning. So my mother went out to work on Saturdays and some evenings, either to cook or to clean. On the Saturdays I would scrub the kitchen floor, black and polish the kitchen grate, and polish the knives, so that my mother could have a little rest on her return from several hours cleaning, sometimes having to walk at least a mile to her regular place of work.

The war was an anxious time, for the daily newspapers were

11

filled with the lists of men killed in the battles in France, and we lived in daily dread of the routine telegram from the War Office. Father was invalided out before the end of the war with a poisoned hand, and a year after his return my youngest brother was born, there being over seventeen years difference in our ages. My mother insisted on my being one of his godfathers, a unique responsibility which has allowed me to offer him some tactful advice from time to time.

From the age of seven I had always wanted to be a missionary and I well remember my mother returning from a missionary meeting in the village to hear me say that was what I hoped one day to be. The hope persisted, though often it seemed impossible. The clergy at our parish church of St Luke, Maidenhead, encouraged the hope. The vicar, Charles Fry, taught me elementary Greek on Saturdays in my latter years at school, and in return I wrote some letters at his dictation, for which he generously gave me a shilling an hour. A curate at St Luke's, an older man from the West Indies, almost persuaded my parents to let me go out to Codrington College in the West Indies, but my headmaster was firm against this, expressing the hope that I might get a scholarship to an English university.

The hope of the scholarship meant specialising. I would have liked to specialise in classics or literature, but the teachers of these two subjects were away at the war, so it was necessary to take up mathematics which the headmaster himself taught. I had passed the London Matriculation in all the necessary subjects for Oxford, Cambridge and London. Finally Selwyn College, Cambridge offered me a scholarship, Berkshire County Council doubled this amount, and the Ordination Candidates Fund made up the two hundred pounds per annum necessary for university life in 1921. Looking back I am increasingly grateful to the many people who took a share in this fortunate happening, though now I realise that I might have expressed my gratitude to them more often and more appreciatively.

CHAPTER 2

Getting Shaped

I went up to Cambridge in the Michaelmas term of 1921. Selwyn was the smallest of the colleges of the University, also its students lived in, and during my three years the number of students never exceeded 150. For some reason known only to the Fellows I was nominated as senior of the four scholars of my year. Roughly half of the students came from public schools and the other half from county or secondary schools. I soon discovered that those in the first group had a poise and confidence that the rest of us did not. They seemed to have a different attitude to the lecturers and were not afraid to go to them for elucidation of points they did not fully understand, and in tutorials showed their wider knowledge, and their readiness to think for themselves rather than just reproduce what they had learned from textbooks and lectures.

The college authorities did not aim solely or mainly for brilliant scholars or outstanding athletes, but to develop and train those who were capable of a good pass or honours degree. Looking back I can see that I was somewhat raw material that could benefit from such provision.

The sports clubs were eager to discover promising members. It was soon clear that rowing was not my strong point. At hockey there was a vacancy for the goalkeeper and that had been my position in the school team. I was ultimately awarded colours but in my third year lost my place after a sharp attack of influenza which weakened my confidence. At cricket I played in the second eleven, and was its captain in my third year. In the same year I was elected as president of the Junior Common Room, and presided at debates and business sessions of the student body.

At one point I was able to take an unusual iniative. Unlike most other colleges, Selwyn had a college mission working in city areas which needed social activities in a club or institute. As Selwyn had been founded to commemorate the great Bishop of Melanesia it seemed appropriate that the college should make Melanesia its special interest and perhaps in time raise enough money to pay one of its own men to go out and serve as priest and educationist in that diocese of so many islands. However at a recent annual Commemoration I was glad to discover that the offerings of the two services are still sent to the Melanesian Mission.

Cambridge is conveniently close to Newmarket and a group of friends went to watch several of the great races there. In my final year the same group decided to have a little flutter on the Derby. Each of us invested ten shillings and we met to decide our bets. We placed bets on three horses, then decided to allow the gyp or college servant who placed the bets for us to make his own choice for the same amount as each of our three bets. Finally, I suppose to salve our consciences, we put the same bet each way on a horse for Dr Barnardo's Homes. When the results became known, we found that our own bets were lost, but the gyp made a handsome winning and Dr Barnardo's did quite well. When I wrote to Dr Barnardo's, I said that they might not approve of money from such a source but the secretary who answered the letter said he was an old Selwyn man and the more we could send him the better.

After a reasonable second class in Part I of the mathematics Tripos I transferred to theology: my tutor, Fred Marsh, gave me a deep love and critical understanding of the Old Testament, but was realistic about my chances in the theological Tripos. "You are a good second class student," was his verdict; "my job is to help you scrape up enough marks to push you over the border line." He succeeded in doing so, but confided afterwards that no single examiner thought me worthy of a first, but when the marks were added up, mine were within a few marks of those who were obviously in the first class, and so my name was added to the list of three others.

14

Further theological and pastoral training came at St Augustine's Missionary College, Canterbury, where Arthur Knight was Warden, after being invalided home from Burma, where he had been Bishop of Rangoon from 1902 to 1910. Arthur Knight was a scholar, and had been Fellow and Dean of Caius College, Cambridge. He was a man of stern self-discipline, whose highest value was that of truth, not only in word, but in thought and theological study. He was also one of the humblest of men. *"Tapeinosis*, my dear Appleton; be humble, be humble," was said to me a score of times, and I imagine to many another student. My wife and children have felt that their vocation in life was to carry on this early training so that I have had a lifetime's pressure towards humility, reinforced by the effect of biblical meditation and involvement in the worship of the Church.

It was a rule at St Augustine's College that the part of the world to which each student should go should be decided by the Warden and Fellows. Signs were not lacking of my probable destiny. I had been enrolled as a student at Canterbury before I went to Cambridge; during the next four years I was visited by missionaries home on leave from Burma, though nothing definite was said. Towards the end of my last year I was called by Bishop Knight and asked where I would like to serve. I replied with caution and a slightly playful evasion that I understood that he would decide that, to which he replied that naturally he would like to take into account any hopes of mine. When I mentioned Burma, his feeling of satisfaction was obvious, though his sense of integrity had prevented him from deciding that I should go to a country so close to his own heart.

But before Burma I was to serve a curacy in East London at Stepney parish church for two years. Here, in addition to a solid training and discipline for a priest, I was to get a widening and somewhat disturbing understanding of the task of a missionary. At Canterbury the students were given very little direct teaching about other faiths, and what there was seemed designed to show that Christianity was the only true religion and that the fate of people of other religions was to be absorbed in a triumphalist

Church. In Stepney 40 per cent of the parishioners were Jews, and almost in the first week I was to become aware of something new, when the rector, Bertram Simpson, later Bishop of Southwark, suddenly said to me, "Tomorrow is the Day of Atonement. You had better attend the closing hour of it in the synagogue in Rectory Square. I will arrange it with my friend, the rabbi. Don't forget to wear a hat!" So next day I duly went to the synagogue, rather self-conscious in my trilby hat, surprised to find women sitting in the gallery only, much impressed with the singing of the cantor and the blowing of the ram's horn, and a little taken aback by the quick exit at the end of the fast, presumably to get back home for the first square meal of the day.

But the thing that impressed me most was the friendship between the rabbi and the rector. They gave each other presents at the Hanukha-Christmas festival, and the rector showed me his latest gift, a book with the inscription "To my friend the rector, from his friend, the rabbi".

During my crowded two years at Stepney, the Church of England Missionary Council initiated a study of world religions. For the East London course, speakers were sent from Church House to be responsible for the study of Hinduism and Islam, but no one was available for Buddhism and Confucianism. My missionary vocation landed me with the task; the experience probably did more for me than for the fifty to one hundred loyal missionary supporters who attended. The study of the Buddha made me feel that I was in the presence of a very great religious teacher, a man of great compassion, who diagnosed man's original trouble as greed, desire, attachment, the escape from which was the treading of the Noble Eightfold Path. In Confucius and his teaching about right relationships – parent-child, teacher-pupil, ruler-subject, man and his neighbour, I saw the presentation of the cultured Chinese ideal of learning, virtue and duty. Neither of these two great figures said much about God, the Buddha being involved in the human situation, and Confucius in the cultural. Living five hundred years before Christ, when there was not much in the way of religious encounter between the Middle East and the Further East, their spiritual greatness and the influence they exerted on the people of their own area and era, raised questions in the mind of any would-be missionary. But the question was being only vaguely suggested – the next forty-five years would see it become more sharply pointed, demanding an answer from the interested individual and from the missionary Church. In October 1927, the young missionary was steaming at 15-20 knots towards Rangoon. In the early-morning sun the incomparably beautiful Shwe Dagon pagoda with its gold-plated spire could be seen from some miles away.

I was to serve at St Michael's church, Kemmendine, a suburb of Rangoon, where there was a parish church, a teachers' training school and a blind school. Kemmendine was the headquarters of a large rural mission in the delta of the Irrawaddy, with some forty villages where there were groups of Christians, mainly Karens; but some Burman. In most of these villages there would be a small one-teacher school, built of wood and bamboo with palm leaf thatching. With smaller Christian groups the school would also be used as a church, but several larger communities had separate churches, built in the same way.

At Kemmendine, there were two experienced missionaries, men of outstanding ability, character and devotion. The first was William Purser who over twenty-five years had built up the Delta mission, originated work for the blind, organised teacher-training and supervised the small theological school of the diocese. A day or two after my arrival he said to me, "In nine months' time I am retiring from missionary service. During that time I shall give you no set work, you are to take no services in English nor preach in English, your sole task will be to become competent in Burmese. The Sunday after I leave, I shall expect you to preach in depth and at reasonable length! I shall find you a good language teacher, and second a catechist, to take you round the villages and ensure that you can converse with Christians and Buddhists alike."

I had made a start in Burmese at the School of Oriental Languages in London, going up from Stepney for a weekly lesson, so I could read haltingly and use a score or more greetings and

17

questions, which deceived the kindly village people into thinking that I knew more than I did, with the result that an opening sentence of mine would elicit a whole string of Burmese from which I would only pick up a word or two. However, Will Purser helped me with a few defensive sentences such as, "Please talk slowly, I have only just begun to learn Burmese." He also gave me his own way of planning little dialogues, and his technique of distinguishing the three tones of the language, which could alter the meaning of what looked to an English eye to be the same word, often with unexpected, humorous or even disastrous effect. Will was a man of self-discipline and order, and also one of quiet, confident calm which nothing seemed to shake, mishaps being greeted with a reassuring acceptance and often a laugh.

The second early influence came from his brother-in-law, William Jackson, a blind priest, who had joined him to develop the work among the blind. William Jackson, always called "Father", *A-pay-gee* (big father) in Burmese, had done an amazing job in giving confidence to his blind pupils, reducing Burmese to Braille, planning weaving, making baskets and mats of all descriptions. He was a very high churchman, preferring Roman ways of worship, though reserving the right to make changes of his own. He loved his blind boys, taught them how to play football, arranged sports days for them, took them swimming. He trained them to regular confession, and whenever any one of them was dying would prepare them for death, and be thankful when they died in penitence, peace and hope.

He taught me two things in addition to the pastoral spirit. The first was how to use the various organs of speech to pronounce Burmese correctly, for the vowels were pure, some consonants unaspirated, and there was always the tonal complication. The second thing I welcomed from him was the need to get away from outward Western forms in worship and adopt meaningful indigenous forms. So at baptism, the new Christian would be immersed and go down into the river or the immersion font in Burmese skirt and coat, and on emerging from the water be clothed with the three garments of a Burmese monk, only white in colour instead of saffron, this signifying acceptance as a mature member of the religious community and the cleansing from sin.

In church, his flock would sit cross-legged on mats, and touch the ground with their foreheads at moments of deep worship. For preaching he would sit cross-legged on the chancel step, there would be bells to make up in sound what was missing in sight, and incense to enlist a further sense. We shared the one church, but the mission side of worship was western – the two ways continuing independent, like Roman and Celt in early British Christianity. *A-pay-gee* and I agreed to unify our rites. We booted out the pews, the pulpit, the kneeling desks, had Burmese lacquer altar frontals, did away with the alms bags and their seasonal colours and used a monk's begging bowl instead. But we forgot to dispose of the discarded furnishings, and six months later when I went to spend a few days with a senior Burmese colleague, he showed me with great satisfaction his small-town church, furnished with the discarded pews, pulpit, litany desks, with the collection bags being changed according to the ecclesiastical season! It is not always the missionary who is reluctant to change outward forms.

I had a further powerful incentive to learning the language, for SPG, the missionary society which supported me and thirty or more other missionaries in Burma, men and women, had a rule that no missionary could marry before passing the first two language examinations. I was in love before I left England and the hope of marriage was such a spur that with help from the two Williams, I was able to pass with distinction not only two, but three exams. However, credit must also be given to Saya Yàwshu (*Saya* means teacher), the seconded catechist, who for my first year followed me like a shadow, to enlarge my vocabulary and lengthen my conversations and sermons. (My first sermon in Burmese, delivered very slowly, took just over three minutes!) I came to believe that Yàwshu must have been descended from the importunate widow, for he seldom left me alone in those early months, and I was glad to crawl under my mosquito net at night, only to be woken at earliest dawn by my faithful and dutiful friend.

The lady I hoped to marry was Miss Marjorie Alice Barrett, who was a teacher in the National school of St Luke's, Maidenhead, which I had attended when the family moved up from Somerset, and from which I gained a free place to the local county school. We had first got to know one another as young teachers in the parish Sunday schools and in the Band of Hope, where we both signed the pledge against any intoxicating drink, a pledge withdrawn when we became adults.

Her family, like mine, was a respectable working-class one, her father being the groundsman at a private preparatory school. We both took part in Christmas plays and also in temperance plays. After the Epiphany play of 1922 we were taking the home-made costumes back to the storage centre when I suddenly became aware of what an attractive, lovable person she was. When our storage duties were done we shook hands and I drew her to me and kissed her. Her response was, "Oh George, you mustn't!"

I was able to follow up that evening, for my father gave me a lovely chrysanthemum bloom from his greenhouse and the next day I took it to her home and asked her mother, who opened the door to my rather nervous knock, if she would give it to her daughter. Her response was, "You'd better come in and give it to her yourself." From that day on, our future together was assured.

Language exams and medical tests duly proved no obstacle and in September 1929 Madge (as her family called her) sailed from Birkenhead and arrived in Rangoon on 1st October, having politely declined a proposal of marriage on the way out.

We were married in Rangoon cathedral on 3rd October. Bishop Tubbs presided at the service. Madge was attended by six little Burmese bridesmaids, who as soon as she arrived started off up the long aisle, and she followed with the kind friend at whose house she had spent the previous two nights and who "gave her away".

One little oversight became apparent in the service. Madge and

I had discussed beforehand whether or not she should promise to obey her husband, and had agreed that this promise should be omitted. There were several clergy taking part in the service, but we had only one 1928 Revised Prayer Book, which was passed round. Bishop Tubbs did not have this copy in his hand and so asked the 1662 question, and Madge was asked if she would obey. She kindly said she would, but we both used a spiritual eraser to delete that particular phrase. In our fifty years together we both worked out plans and decisions without any friction.

CHAPTER 3

Curry and Rice

My main task in my first five years in Burma was to tour
the villages of the Irrawaddy Delta, encouraging the
small Anglican congregations and visiting some forty
village schools, most of them having only one or two teachers.
The teachers had been trained at two training colleges in Kemmendine, those for primary schools studying for one year and
those for middle schools for two years. There was very little in
the way of school equipment, the children sat on the floor with
slates and chalk, reading books had to be shared and the rough
blackboard made on the spot. In many cases the school was also
the church, where the small groups of Christians, almost entirely
Karen in race, gathered for Sunday worship and for Holy
Communion when I was able to turn up, or occasionally one of
my four Karen "curates". The Karens were animists, feeling some
kind of presence in the forest, the spring or the great banyan tree.
They had some beliefs and practices that seemed to link with the
early days of the Old Testament, possibly due to some earlier
Christian influence, believed by some missionaries to trace back
to Nestorian missionaries moving through parts of Burma into
China. Whatever it was, it gave them a sense of reverence, and
services in these little churches always had a great spirit of
worship. If a Karen died away from home, his body would be
buried and later his bones would be brought back to his native
village. We missionaries were rather slow to respect this return
to the home village by a second funeral service, though in my
time it became more acceptable.

There were no doctors in the villages and the town centres of
government administration were far away. Infectious diseases

came regularly – smallpox, dysentery, malaria, cholera; and in addition there were the regular happenings – broken limbs, snake bite, toothache, injury from treading on a sharp bamboo or from a misdirected blow from the *dah*, a long chopper-knife which every family kept for domestic and jungle use. So the missionary had to try to take the place of the doctor and the nurse, and had to keep with him a stock of basic medicines – iodine, castor oil, Epsom salts, santonin (for worms), quinine tablets for malaria, and a plentiful supply of aspirin in which the village people seemed to have a great faith.

Cholera epidemics happened regularly in my early years, when the filth from one village would be thrown into the river and water drawn from the same river for the villages downstream. In such epidemics we tried to get people to boil their water and to eat their food hot from the rice and curry pots, but it was rare for cholera victims to recover. No one was able to give us at that time the valuable advice which I only picked up years later, namely that the great danger in cholera was dehydration, necessitating that the sufferer be given frequent drinks of cold water previously boiled.

I well remember my first Christmas in Burma. I had gone to a town about a hundred miles north of Rangoon and had spent Christmas night in a village seventeen miles away. We had had our Christmas Communion and the Nativity play which every Christian village made up and acted on Christmas evening. I had gone to bed when shortly after midnight I was wakened by the teacher to say that one of the elders of the village was in great pain. I enquired what seemed to be wrong, and after a little embarrassing silence was told that he was suffering from a stoppage of urine. Stones in the bladder were a very common ailment in middle life, and something for which my first aid training had given me no preparation. I hurried to the house of the sick man, which was a bamboo hut with a palm leaf roof like the schoolroom in which I was sleeping. Somehow I had picked up the idea that putting the patient in a tub of hot water sometimes had the desired effect. We duly did this, with no result. My next thought was that the stone might be closing the outlet from the bladder. So several of us tried standing him on his head and quickly reversing him. Again no result. The only thing left to do was to get him in to the government hospital seventeen miles away, so we set out across the rice fields and village tracks, with the patient in a bullock cart. The teacher and I preferred to walk, for bullock carts had no springs and the tracks were rough. It was a lovely starlit night and except for anxiety for the sufferer a pleasant journey. We had not been going for more than half an hour when the driver of the sick man's bullock cart came to me and said that all was now well, we need go no further. What the hot water and applied gymnastics had failed to do had been achieved by the rough journey in the bullock cart. However, I insisted that we should get him to hospital and soon after dawn we arrived at Prome, where after considerable appeal and importunity on my part the patient was admitted to hospital. That evening while wandering round the bazaar I was suddenly greeted with great friendliness by the erstwhile sufferer, who announced that he was now all right and was going back to his village next morning. I warned him that the trouble would probably recur, but with a smile he said, "If it does, I will go for another ride in a bullock cart!"

One of the things that bothered me most in the villages of the Delta was the treatment given to women in childbirth. This was undertaken by one of the more experienced older women who had little understanding of possible complications. To make matters worse it was generally believed that the spirit of the child would remain in the body of the mother, and so for three days after the actual birth the mother had to sit by a wood and bamboo fire and sweat out the child's spirit so that the child should be completed and the mother freed from what was now an alien spirit inside her. I could do little to help in this experience of childbirth except to urge that the mother should be kept in her rough bed on the floor and given proper nourishment. But centuries-old practices are difficult to change, and my protests were written off as those of an ignorant missionary, with no respect for traditional customs.

Relief came more quickly than my troubled heart expected, for it had been decided that the matron of the SPG hospital at Mandalay could be spared for rural medical work. I jumped at the offer and within a week or two she arrived and reform was started. After seeing what Avice Cam could do, we decided to plan a long-term revolution. A small hospital built of wood and bamboo and thatched with palm leaves, with one ward for about ten beds, a labour room and a room for Avice, was built, and six village girls agreed to come for training. News of the care and comfort supplied to mother and child soon got round and there was no need to go out and persuade pregnant women to come in to have their babies. After a year's training the village nurses were placed in local dispensaries and went to look after mothers in childbirth in their own homes. Avice Cam deserved the highest honour that could be given for service to others. She was a woman of fine physical strength, ready to go out on foot or in a canoe when called for. Her service demanded more than just strength and devotion, for she had a most sensitive skin which attracted mosquitoes and during the rainy season and its close, was constantly itching and scratching. Years later when I became chairman of the medical missions of SPG, I realised how in mission hospitals all over the world, the same devoted healing mission was being carried on, which spoke much more eloquently of divine and human love than the preaching of less qualified friends like myself.

People in the villages were poor. They grew their own rice and a surplus for sale, and often the villagers were able to catch fish from the many streams of the Irrawaddy Delta. But clothes had to be bought, and medicines, and cooking pots and kerosene for the hurricane lamps. Life generally was hard. Some pattern of what might be done needed to be worked out, and after a great deal of discussion and searching for funds, we transferred one of the men's teacher training classes from Kemmendine to a Delta village. The new training school was built as a village with school and church and shop. The students had not only training in teaching methods but in growing their own food, and we had twenty acres of rice land, an acre of garden, a Berkshire boar imported to improve the strength and size of the village pigs, and several pure-bred cocks to convert the village hens from laying two clutches of a dozen eggs each year to something like 150 bigger and better eggs. The Berkshire boar attracted great attention, and was given the name Norman, after our bishop, Norman Tubbs. He was somewhat taken aback by this honour and we were quick to explain that this was the finest tribute that could be paid to both Normans. Sows were brought from miles around for mating, while settings of eggs were supplied for broody village hens, who were never fed but had to pick up their food from the village or the rice field. Another devoted woman missionary, Phoebe England, did the professional training, while a third noble woman continued touring the other villages and linking them up with the training village. In such ways we learned to care for people's bodies and homes as well as for their inner spiritual life.

To someone recently out from England village life in Burma seemed desperately poor. It was only when I got to know something of the poverty of India's villages (some 500,000 of them) that I really saw far worse poverty. As I learned more of missionary work all over the world, I began to realise that there had to be a tremendous effort to help undernourished people to grow their own food for themselves, a task which is still tragically unfinished, and will remain so until the nations of the world, rich and poor, combine together to sacrifice a meagre percentage of their gross national product, which experts calculate to be necessary to abolish hunger in a generation. But, thank God, we now have the UN Food and Agriculture Organisation, and the World Health Organisation, but alas, are still waiting for the developed countries to engage in this world-wide task.

CHAPTER 4

The Smile of the Buddha

I have visited many countries in the world and can think of no
other which can compare with Burma for the permeation of
its cultural and social life with religion. Everywhere there were
reminders of Buddhism: on almost every hill there would be a
small pagoda, its graceful, tapering spire coloured white or
occasionally gilded with gold leaf; in every village there would
be a monastery, usually with several monks, though sometimes
with a single *bhikkhu* living more as a hermit. The monks used to
be responsible for the education of the boys, teaching them the
three Rs and the elements of Buddhism, the learning being almost
entirely by rote, so that approaching a village one could often
hear from a distance the shrill boyish voices as they repeated the
lesson after their teacher. Every Buddhist boy became a monk for
a period, it might be for a lent, or a year or two, it might continue
for a lifetime or be as short as a week. Until he had undergone
this religious initiation and probation he would not be regarded
as a mature member of the Buddhist community. It did not
take me long to wish that we Christians might have a similar
preparation for confirmation and acceptance as a full worshipping
and working member of the Church. Every day there would be
a reminder of religious dedication, for each morning the monks
would process round the village or town in file, carrying their
begging bowls into which devout Buddhists would put offerings
of food, very respectfully and without expecting any thanks, for
supporting the monks was a most meritorious deed.

In addition there would be religious festivals, a commemoration
of some event in the life of the Buddha, or the founding of a
monastery, sometimes even a commemoration of the appearance

of a *nat* or spirit, and interestingly the funeral of a monk, a time of great rejoicing and festivity, for had not the holy man entered Nirvana, and he would return no more to the wearisome cycle of human rebirths.

William Purser was very wise. He left me to become acquainted with the religious environment, and then handed me a paperback entitled *Modern Buddhism in Burma*, which he had edited in cooperation with Kenneth Saunders, warden of the YMCA hostel, and already a translator of the *Dhamma-pada*, a collection of short sayings thought to go back to the Buddha. This book of 100 pages consisted of an edited summary of answers to a questionnaire which the two editors had sent out not only to missionaries but also to Buddhist laymen and government officials. It was inspired by the report of the Edinburgh Missionary Conference of 1910, which set in motion the new ecumenical movement among the Christian Churches. The official report of that conference expressed regret at the omission of any adequate treatment of Southern Buddhism, and the questionnaire and its answers attempted to remedy the omission. It aimed at understanding contemporary Buddhism, and deprecated any intention of an attack on Buddhism, appealing to Buddhist readers to correct any inaccurate or biased statements.

I was impressed with the open mind which the writers brought to their task, though their missionary motive could not be hidden. The survey also made me realise that it was not enough to have read about the early beginnings of any religion; one needed to study it as a living faith and see the development of thought and interpretation.

This report, the standard books, the growing number of translations of the many books of the Scriptures, and discussions with scholars in Rangoon University or simple yet thoughtful Buddhists in the villages, aroused in me a reverent admiration for the Buddha, a deep interest in his teaching, and a nagging need to build some bridge in my own mind between the two religions.

The return of William Purser to England released me from my obligation not to preach in English, and shortly after his departure

I was invited to preach in Rangoon cathedral, then very much a chaplaincy parish church, and only rarely having great services in Burmese. I chose as my subject the person of the Buddha, tried to relate his teaching to Christians, expressed my deep admiration for him and pleaded for a more tolerant and positive attitude towards the religion which he had founded.

Further sympathetic understanding came through the study of two books by Mrs C.A.F. Rhys Davids. With her husband she had taken an active part in the publications of the Pali Text Society, both in Pali, the classical language of Buddhism, and in English. The two books were *Gotama the Man* (sometimes spelt Gautama), and a splendidly substantial one entitled *Sakya*. On my first furlough I sought her out, and attended her course of lectures. I was excitedly interested in her attempt to get back to the original Gautama, instead of the stereotyped figure of the Scriptures and Buddhist tradition, and still more thrilled by her insistence that the Buddha had a gospel, good news to the people of his contemporary India and to later generations.

What was that gospel? It was expressed in the Four Noble Truths, which may be paraphrased as: 1) Human life is characterised by frustration, meaninglessness, suffering. 2) The cause of this is desire, attachment, greed. 3) Desire must and can be stopped. 4) The way to achieve this is by following the Noble Eightfold Path – right views, right thought, right speech, right actions, right employment, right mental discipline, right endeavour, right meditation.

So there is a way of escape, a cessation of desire, an achievement of ineffable peace and blessedness. Men are the product of their past thoughts and deeds, according to the working of the law of karma, the harvest of deeds; as a man sows so shall he reap, a principle accepted by St Paul in Galatians, a nexus of cause and effect. But men are not in the hands of blind fate, for karma speaks not only of the actions and thoughts of the past as explaining a man's present condition or character, but also as creative of the future. Do good deeds now and the result will be a future of happiness and blessing. The Buddha warned men not to rely on mantras, incantations, sacrifices, rites and ceremonies; he insisted that they cannot be saved without their own co-operation. They must be creative workers for their own future.

According to the Thera-vada school of Buddhism, the Southern Buddhism of Burma, Ceylon, Siam and Cambodia, there is no grace from outside man's being to support, strengthen and save him; he must rely on his own efforts, and the task will need more lives than one, countless lives in this world, alternating perhaps with lives in a heaven or hell. Buddhists of the Northern school of China and Japan evolved their own theory of grace and came to believe in the Buddha as a Saviour, though in the earliest Scriptures he himself claimed to be nothing more than a teacher, a show-er of the way.

The Buddhist goal is Nirvana, which some Western writers have thought of as completely negative, annihilation or nothingness. The word itself means "blown out", "cool", meaning that the fires of desire, hatred and illusion have been extinguished, the heat of desire has become cool. The Buddha did not define it, but a modern Buddhist scholar, Edward Conze, has summarised references from the Scriptures in the following moving description:

> We are told that Nirvana is permanent, stable, imperishable, unmovable, ageless, deathless, unborn and unbecome; that it is power, bliss and happiness, the secure refuge, the shelter and the place of unassailable safety, that it is the real truth and the Supreme Reality; that it is the Good, the Supreme goal, and the one and only consummation of our life, the eternal, hidden and incomprehensible Peace.

Christians could apply almost all these attributes to God himself, in which Nirvana becomes the presence of God. As Psalm 16:11 says, "In thy presence is fulness of joy; in thy right hand bliss for evermore." Nirvana, like eternal life in the teaching of Jesus, can be attained in this life, as it was in the case of the Buddha who consented to stay on in this world for the sake of men, rather than move on at once to Para-nirvana, the final and highest heaven.

Inevitably Buddhists and Christians compare Gautama the Buddha and Jesus the Christ. Both had a great compassion for men in their frustrations, sufferings and lostness. Both underwent deep spiritual experience before they embarked on their public ministry, the Buddha in his night of illumination under the Bo tree when he discovered a way of escape for men from suffering, and the Christ in the forty days in the harsh countryside of the Dead Sea, when he was shown and accepted the way of love, sacrifice and service, as the way of salvation in the Kingdom of God. Both trained bands of disciples and sent them out to preach their respective good news. Both made great sacrifices – the Buddha by consenting to live, and the Christ by being willing to die. Both were prophetically critical of the religions in which they were nurtured, the Buddha in Indian religion, and the Christ in Judaism. Both aroused the opposition of the traditional teachers, the brahmins in Hinduism and the rabbis in Judaism, though it was their adherents in following generations who heightened the differences until they resulted in complete separation and the founding of two new religions.

There were vital differences. The Buddha discouraged speculation about the origin of things, about the existence of God and the soul in man. He wanted men to go on with living the good life. To Jesus God was the great reality and the essential priority. He believed that he came from God, revealed God, spoke for God, acted for God, was a channel for God's grace and salvation.

"There is only one whom we might be inclined to compare with Jesus: Buddha. This man is a great mystery. He lived in an almost super-human freedom, yet his kindness was powerful as a cosmic force. Perhaps Buddha will be the last religious genius to be explained by Christianity." These words of Monsignor Guardini, written nearly thirty years after my early musings, expressed a growing need in my thinking to account for the Buddha in the providence of God. "God was in Christ, reconciling the world to himself," says St Paul. Can we not say that "God

31

was in the Buddha, teaching men the way of virtue and righteous-ness", even though the Buddha did not clearly acknowledge God?

Bishop B.F. Westcott in his book *The Gospel of Life*, written in 1892, had a paragraph which comes near to this crystallisation:

> Buddhism started with being morality without worship; and it is as a system of morality, but of morality as being of inherent obligation, that Buddhism claims to be reckoned among the religions of the world. In this respect it is among the noblest as it is the vastest moral spectacle in history.

May it not be the mission of Buddhism today to lead the world back to moral values and to help people everywhere to find an ethic, related to conditions in the modern world, which will gain acceptance and inspire right effort?

Yet the Buddha had an ultimate in which he believed:

> There is, monks, an unborn not become, not made, un-compounded, and were it not, monks, for this unborn, not become, not made, uncompounded, no escape could be shown here, for what is born, has become made, is com-pounded. But because there is, monks, an unborn, not become, not made, uncompounded, therefore an escape be shown for what is born, has become, is made, is com-pounded.

In short, there is an eternal into which men can be liberated, suggesting something which exists in its own right and is not dependent on any prior cause. When I first came across this text my mind went to the Athanasian Creed which describes the Godhead as uncreated, infinite, eternal and incomprehensible.

The Buddha spoke often and at length to his disciples about what he called *dhamma* (the Pali word for the Sanskrit *dharma*). Dhamma is the principle of order in the universe, truth in both cosmic and inner sense, a manifestation of ultimate truth, reality. It is something other, independent, with a dynamic quality of its own, and an initiating activity. Dhamma is a Reality, inwardly seen, not handed down as tradition. An alert monk, says the Buddha, guides his conduct by it.

The Buddha's first sermon after his enlightenment, given in the deer park at Banaras, is entitled "The Turning of the Wheel of Dhamma". When he sent out his disciples he instructed them to preach Dhamma, the Truth, the Norm. "The gift of dhamma", says one of the pithy sayings in the Dhamma-pada (verses about dhamma), "exceeds all gifts; its sweetness exceeds all sweetness"; reminding the Christian of Psalm 19 where the Torah, the Law of the Lord, is described as "sweeter than honey".

When the Buddha lay dying, his devoted attendant Ananda asked for instructions about the *Sangha*, the Order of Monks. The master replied that he had ever taught dhamma, and dhamma must be their light and guide: "Therefore, Ananda, dwell making yourselves your island, making yourselves, not anyone else, your refuge; making dhamma your island, dhamma your refuge, nothing else your refuge." Earlier, the Buddha had said, "He who sees dhamma sees me, he who sees me sees dhamma."

They are to depend on dhamma only, revere dhamma, esteem dhamma, with dhamma as their banner, with dhamma as their guard and protection, with mastery in dhamma.

Dhamma is for awakening, for taming, for calming, for crossing over, for utter Nirvana.

Dhamma is the charioteer that drives the chariot along the road to Nirvana. In other references dhamma is the raft on which men may cross the ocean of existence to the farther shore of Nirvana.

Dhamma is the master principle in "a *Tathagata*, perfected one, wholly awakened one, a dhamma-man, a dhamma-king, depending on dhamma only, honouring dhamma, revering dhamma, esteeming dhamma, with dhamma as his standard, with dhamma as his banner, with mastery as to dhamma", and he will provide dhamma-guard, love and protection for monks, nuns and lay followers. He will do this by teaching the right kind of deeds, speech and thought, the right way of living, even the right places to visit or live in.

33

A Christian may relate this concept to that of the Word in the prologue to St John's Gospel, or to the idea of Wisdom in the Old Testament and the Apocrypha with its quasi-personal cause. He will be reminded of the saying of Jesus, "He who has seen me has seen the Father." In the growing meeting of religions, he will want to discuss with Buddhist friends the possibility of equating dhamma with the Christian concept of God, though without the personal elements. He will examine more confidently his own intuition and hope, that there is Something or Somebody at work behind the scenes in all religions.

Thera-vada Buddhism, the Buddhism of the Elders, has no belief in a soul or entity in man. If belief in an Ultimate develops, belief in a self will not be difficult. There is, however, help from Buddhism itself. The Buddha deprecated argument about whether there is an *atman* or self in man. He wanted people to get on with the urgent business of living the good life set out in the Eightfold Path, and not to waste time or energy in speculation and debate. He taught that the natural order of things was marked by three characteristics:

> *dukkha*, suffering, frustration, meaninglessness
> *a-neissa*, impermanent, not eternal
> *an-atta*, no self, no soul, non-substantiality.

The question arises as to what he was describing – ultimate reality or the life of men? Was he really saying that blessedness, permanence and true being had to be sought elsewhere?

According to Buddhists the constituents of being are the five *Khandas* – form or body, feeling, perception, mental activity and consciousness. When these five aggregates are in combination, there is life, a being is in existence, though the aggregates themselves are always changing. When they disintegrate death takes place. The Thera-vada deduction from this is that there is no self. Might not the Buddha have been saying that the self is none of these constituents, nor all of them in combination, but something other, something that owns, uses and directs these faculties? This is a question which we in the West need to ask ourselves, for too often we identify the self with the body, or feeling or thinking or consciousness. What happens when we sleep or are unconscious? Is there not a deep self that keeps active in the subconscious, expressing in dreams the thoughts that it evades in conscious life?

There are references to a self in the Scriptures attributed to the Buddha. In one of the poems of the early Buddhist saints there occur the following two stanzas:

> Within this little five-doored hut an ape
> Doth prowl, and round and round from door to door
> He hies, rattling with blows again, again.

> Halt ape! run thou not forth. For thee
> 'Tis not herein as it was wont to be,
> Wisdom doth hold thee captive. Never more
> Shalt roam far hence (in freedom as of yore).

The five doors are clearly the five senses, the restless ape is the ego, but who is it that gives the order "Halt, ape!"?

The Dhamma-pada has two relevant verses:

> Self is the lord of self, who else could be the Lord? With self well subdued, a man finds a Lord such as few can find.

> Rouse thyself by thyself, examine thyself by thyself, thus self-protected and attentive wilt thou live happily, O monk.
> For self is the lord of self,
> self is the refuge of self,
> therefore curb thyself as the merchant curbs a noble horse.

A passage reminiscent of the Buddha's final word to Ananda. There is clearly a self which needs to be repudiated, an ever-changing, superficial, grasping, possessive thing, the stream of feelings, thoughts and desires, which insists on taking over the direction of life. This is surely the self spoken of in modern terms as the ego, the lower nature which St Paul urges Christians to crucify, so that the true self, created by God and nourished by the Spirit of Christ, may take over.

So there is much for Buddhists and Christians to discuss together, much indeed for Buddhists to discuss among themselves, for in the early days there was a group of *atta-vadins*, people who believed in a self, while in Maha-yana, the Buddhism of the north, a more developed doctrine of salvation and grace would seem to make belief in selfhood logical.

Another point at which Buddhist and Christian thought touch is in their respective views of what is wrong with man. I cannot do better than quote a semi-paragraph from *The Grail Legend* by Emma Jung and Marie Louise Von Franz (English translation 1971):

> The growth of consciousness about myself proceeds simultaneously with an awareness of guilt. This realisation is already expressed in the bible story of Paradise, providing the occasion for the concept of original sin, as well as the Eastern belief in Karma, equivalent to a debt that has to be paid, which the individual brings with him into his present life.

Buddhists believe that Gautama the Buddha was the successor to a long line of earlier Buddhas, all distinguished by shrewdness, wisdom, love or sacrifice. Many believe that there is a final Buddha still to come, who will be the Buddha of Love, as Gautama was the Buddha of enlightenment and wisdom. This final Buddha is known as *Maitri, Maitreya* or *Arimaddeyya*. In the answers to the questionnaire circulated by Purser and Saunders, a monk living among the Shans near the Chinese border described the transformation which would take place when the Maitri Buddha comes: "the mountains will be levelled and world become a vast plain full of orchards, gardens and rice fields. Man then will be without an enemy among men and without fear of ravening beasts. It will be an age of plenty and good will." This winsome description fits in with the descriptions of the messianic age in the book of Isaiah, with the wolf lying down with the lamb, the lion and the ox eating straw together, and the little child playing happily and fearlessly with them and even putting its little hand unhurt into the hole of the poisonous viper.

Buddhists with this expectation of Maitri, Jews with their longing for the messianic age, Christians with their hope of the second coming of Christ, can talk together about the golden age ahead – their respective eschatologies, their glimpses of an eternal city, the abiding home of the human spirit.

Reviewing my years in Burma, it is I hope clear how one who went out to preach a gospel also heard another gospel, a complementary one, and learned from the gentle, tolerant Buddhists of Burma something close to what the Buddha tried to teach.

CHAPTER 5

Strengthening the Foundations

J ust before I went on my first furlough after five years' service, the Bishop of Rangoon, Norman Tubbs, called me and told me that on my return from furlough he wanted me to take over the training of the Burmese clergy. He had previously appointed me as an examining chaplain, as most of the duties involved were in connection with the ordination of European clergy. The training of the vernacular clergy had been in the hands of Arthur Dilworth, the first time that a missionary had been completely set aside for this important task. Arthur had set up a rural-type training settlement on an island in the middle of the Kokine lake, just outside the university of Rangoon. Under the bishop's plan he and I were to change places, and while I was on furlough he was to keep both jobs going, and I would do the same on my return. When both of us were back the new arrangements would come into full working.

Another temporary need fitted in to this plan, for Robert Slater, the Anglican chaplain at the university, was also to go on leave, and I was to keep services going in the little wooden Anglican church on the university side of the lake, as well as the other two quite heavy responsibilities.

Out of all this crowded year came the thought that the divinity school might well be accommodated in the ample compound of the university chapel. It was thought that this would stimulate our divinity students in being close to the university and so involved in contact with university students who would in future years be leaders of the nation, just as we hoped the divinity students would become leaders of the Church. When Robert Slater returned he accepted this idea with enthusiasm, and it was he who planned the new hostel and took a very active hand in raising the modest sum necessary for the building. At the same time it was agreed that we should call the divinity school by the name "College of Holy Cross", which would give it added dignity and incentive.

Ths missions, chaplaincies and institutions of the diocese all combined generously to provide the necessary money, grants were secured from SPG and from SPCK, and in just over two years the new building was raised, waiting for the foundation stone to be laid during the opportune visit of the Metropolitan of Calcutta, the Most Reverend Foss Westcott, son of the famous biblical scholar and bishop of Durham.

While on furlough in England my thoughts had naturally been on the new tasks ahead. Missionary interest had been greatly stirred by the work in training ordinands in what was then the Gold Coast, by Dom Bernard Clements OSB. I went to visit him at the Benedictine monastery at Nashdom and asked him for any insights which he could give me from his experience in Accra. He emphasised the need for devotional discipline and training in holiness, and added that in West Africa he had introduced a choir practice on every day of the working week. This immediately caught my imagination, for in the indigenous churches in Burma we had no musical instruments and no choirs. The priest had to act as both choirmaster and precentor, setting the pitch and intoning the first line of each hymn, as well as training his people to sing the Merbecke setting which Father Jackson had adapted for Burmese use. Starting each hymn on the right note was a great problem for most of us, but I found that if I did not think too deeply about this but started off almost instinctively I generally hit something like the right note, thanks to my years as a choir boy in Maidenhead. But there were mistakes and sometimes a wrong tune was precented which did not fit the words, and on one or two occasions the congregation took up a tune of their own which was not intended in my precenting.

Once the new building was in use, we started the daily choir practices. At the same time we began another daily exercise in a period of devotional Bible study. At 9.30 each morning staff and students would meet in the little oratory of the hostel, a completely bare room with just a crucifix on the wall. We followed the Bible Reading Fellowship monthly notes. A student would read the passage for the day, I would explain any background needed and then we would all keep silence for a quarter of an hour to let the Scripture passage make its own impression. We would then spend a few moments sharing any relevant and deep intuition that had come to any of us, and it was remarkable to see what a full and varied message the daily passage gave us.

Before long, the diocese appointed a sub-warden, a Canadian priest with a splendid knowledge of the Old Testament, and a "young" Anglo-Indian priest whose main study had been the New Testamant. Quite a number of the students knew no English when they arrived, and the first year was spent in giving them a working knowledge. The teaching had to be simple and as there was no appropriate textbook, summary notes had to be dictated. I was the only one of the three who had any confidence in Burmese, and so was able to be bilingual in teaching and in giving notes. It was quite an exciting and exacting task to work out the meaning of basic Christian terms, for in Burmese almost all the abstract nouns and religious words came from the religious language of Buddhism.

After five years my two colleagues left, one to return to Canada and the other to become assistant priest at Rangoon cathedral, so I was left to do my best with all the subjects of the curriculum, except for occasional help from visiting clergy or teachers. This one-man effort had its advantages, for it meant that one mind was responsible for the training, rather like the method which our Lord followed with his disciples, or the Buddha with his. It also did me a world of good, for I had to study the basic faith, teaching and life and express it in as simple words as possible. This gave me a deeper basis for my own thinking, devotion and ministry. It meant however that we had little time to relate our studies at any deep level to Buddhism, but it seemed unanswerable that people must have a deep understanding of their own faith before they can go on to study that of other people. However, we were able to study the basic history of Buddhism, the life of the Buddha and the simplified summaries which every Buddhist learns.

The work at Holy Cross became further integrated when Robert Slater became the chaplain of Rangoon cathedral. He had lectured on philosophy in the university and had made numerous friendly contacts which were of great use to myself, though I was unable to follow on his very able lectures to university students. There were two colleges in the university, one a government institution with very able staff, mainly European in my early years, and the other Judson College, founded and maintained by the American Baptist Church which was the biggest Church in Burma. We at Holy Cross were able to have a happy relationship with the Baptists at Judson College, and I was invited to give a regular course in the comparative study of religion, which I attempted to do in the way which would now be described as that of dialogue. The discussions at the end of each lecture were animated and sometimes a little heated, for Hindu students, Muslims and Buddhists were a little critical at having to attend any Christian lecture and were very emphatic that they much preferred their own religion to that of Christianity.

The relationship between staff and students of University College, apart from the pastoral care of the few Anglican students and staff, involved me increasingly in a study of the history and culture of Burma. There was a Burma Research Society in which both Burmese and European scholars took part, and I was able to learn much from its regular lectures and its quarterly journal. My closest friend in the university was Professor B.R. Pearn, first Registrar and then Professor of History. He had been secretary of the BRS and when he went on furlough I was asked to take on his duties. When he returned he became editor, and a year or two later I had to fill in again for his editorial duties. It was a most fruitful involvement and I can never be grateful enough for what I learned about the long history of Burma and the Buddhist culture which was woven into the life of the people.

In 1928 a new Prayer Book had been authorised for use in the

41

Anglican Church in England. Naturally the overseas extensions of the Anglican way of life were interested to revise their own prayer books. The translation of the new book was in the hands of a very scholarly missionary, Charles Garrad, and before long he enlisted me as his assistant. With meticulous care and wide knowledge of Burmese, acquired through years of membership of a Bible translation committee, he bore the main burden, and I received invaluable experience and training. When he left Burma, the task of seeing the new prayer book through the press fell to me. The students at Holy Cross took their share in the very considerable proof-reading, for we included collects, epistles and gospels, which had not been done except by reference in the earlier Burmese prayer books. With a team of proof-readers working together, we did a very competent job and there was hardly a misprint in something like four hundred pages.

The satisfaction with which the new prayer book was received and used quickly resulted in a request that the Burmese hymn book should be revised and enlarged, and I was asked to be the editor and secretary of the small revision committee. We badly needed new hymns, more critically translated, and I, with a Burmese colleague, was able to add something like eighty new hymns. I well remember the first one to be accepted, "Firmly I believe and truly", which was sung for the first time at the dedication of Holy Cross College. Almost all the hymns were just translations of English hymns, working very much on English rhythm and rhyme-principle. We had not the experts in Burmese poetry who were really needed for this task; only a handful of hymns in the true Burmese style were available, and these had been composed earlier by Father Jackson. Following Burmese patterns the lines were usually of four syllables with the rhyme coming back diagonally from the fourth word of the first line to the third of the second, the second of the third and the first of the last line. At the time of this translation we were not sufficiently in touch with Burmese poets and authors or with Buddhist monks, who together might have helped us to be more truly indigenous. However, we did our best at that stage, and perhaps Christian poets in Burmese literature will arise and help our people to produce hymns more satisfying to the Burmese spirit and understandable to our Buddhist friends.

The principle on which students were admitted to the Holy Cross was for testing and training, with no guarantee that they would finally be ordained. In the course of ten years, some fifty students were trained, about half of whom went on to ordination and a few of the others were ordained after my time. We tried to live together in a very simple fashion of worship and life. Staff and students sat on mats on the floor in chapel, meals were taken at little low tables, squatting on very low stools, the food was not luxurious but sufficiently nourishing and appetising. The students came from different races in Burma – a few Burmans, more Karens, a Chin or two, a Kachin and several Anglo-Burmans and one Indian; so living, learning and worshipping together called for and indeed produced a spirit of racial understanding and unity. Of the students in my time, one has since become an archbishop, John Aung Hla; another, John Maung Pe became the first bishop of Akyab, and another who came for a short term of study and an even shorter curacy was John Richardson, the saintly schoolteacher, catechist, priest and bishop in turn of Car Nicobar, where under his influence the whole of the island population, including witch doctors, became Christian.

The Japanese invasion brought an end to this initial stage of Holy Cross; the war years were to be a severe testing of the training given. I look back with great thankfulness to God and deep affection to Holy Cross students for what was a most happy and satisfying central period of my life.

CHAPTER 6

Learning to Pray

One of my most treasured possessions is a small book of prayers and meditations, now very dog-eared and patched up. It was written and circulated privately by Evelyn Underhill for the retreats she gave at Pleshey and elsewhere. An introductory note says that she used to read prayers very slowly with frequent pauses, which led almost instantaneously to prayer. I have forgotten how I picked up my copy, it may have been at a retreat which I was asked to lead at Pleshey. When I discover from time to time this tiny book tucked away in my bookcases, I happily peruse it again and always find something, perhaps unnoticed before, which leads me into deeper and more silent meditation.

Among the many Old Testament characters I learned much from the prophet Elijah. After his sensational (and bloodthirsty?) triumph over the priests of Baal on Mount Carmel, he was told of the threat to his life by Ahab's foreign queen Jezebel, and decided to flee down to the desert around Mount Sinai, the home of many prophets and a place of pilgrimage for many more. On his journey, fearful and probably suffering from reactionary depression, he slept a night under a broom bush, where he dreamed that an angel touched him on the shoulder and bade him rise and eat. As he did so, he found a jar of water and a flat loaf of bread still warm from being baked in the hot ashes. He obeyed the dream voice and then lay down to sleep again. The dream recurred, and this time the voice urged him to "rise and eat lest the journey be too great for thee". He did so, and when he woke next morning felt refreshed and encouraged. The Scripture account says that in the strength of that food he was able to accomplish the journey still many days on. It was not a magical experience, enabling him to go without food for the rest of his flight, but it was a meal for the spirit that kept him nourished and firm in his intention until he reached Horeb the mountain of God (1 Kings 19:1-8).

Christians generally associate this incident with the Eucharist, in which our souls are nourished through all the difficulties and adventures of life. Undoubtedly this is so, but God can nourish the soul in additional ways. Every touch with God and every touch of God can strengthen the soul for the journey through life and cleanse and sanctify and prepare it for life in the world to come. I was often reminded of Elijah's revealing dream, for I often passed the traditional site of the sleep under the broom tree, now commemorated by St Elijah's monastery, halfway between Jerusalem and Bethlehem.

Arrived at Sinai, Elijah sheltered in one of the caves with which the sacred mount is honeycombed. Here he underwent a fourfold experience, the memory of which teaches me more about his experience and the life of prayer. One day as he was meditating in his cave there came an accusing voice within him which he immediately interpreted as a word from God. The voice said reproachfully, "What are you doing here, Elijah?" He poured out his heart about the faithlessness of Israel, his own loyalty to God, his loneliness in his dangerous situation, and a feeling that he alone was left to defend the divine cause. Then there followed four episodes that banished his depression. In the first as he stood at the mouth of the cave, a typhoon burst on the mountainside, bringing rocks crashing down. Elijah was unperturbed by this: "the Lord was not in the wind." A day or two later an earthquake shook the whole area and the same thing happened: "the Lord was not in the earthquake." This was followed by a desert fire. Having lived in Australia for some years and witnessed forest fires, leaping from tree to tree and running along the thin covering of bush and grass, I could enter imaginatively into the prophet's experience. His verdict was, "the Lord was not in the fire!" The writer of the book of Kings then speaks of "a still small voice", and this time Elijah wraps himself in his cloak, and hears the reproaching voice again. "What are you doing here, Elijah?"

A modern translation has "a sound of gentle stillness" instead of the still small voice. Both phrases have spoken to me. The still small voice suggests a quiet listening, a quietening of the noises in the heart, as well as the noises going on outside. The sound of gentle stillness reminds me of a field of ripening corn stirred by a gentle summer breeze, or the sound of waves on a sandy beach, some distance away.

Elijah heard a divine message sending him back to troubled Israel, with intuition as to definite things to do, one of which was to find a successor to carry on the prophetic ministry. So he must have been elderly when this Sinai experience took place. He went back as directed, and found the man he had in mind, who was ploughing his family fields. He placed his own mantle on Elisha's shoulders, who said his farewell to his parents, and became Elijah's companion and understudy, following him faithfully on a journey of farewells, and finally inheriting the mantle which fell off Elijah's shoulders as he was actually or mystically carried off in "a whirlwind into heaven".

The Elijah-Elisha saga made a further deep impression on me. Elisha was a gentler person than his master and proved to be a wise adviser to the kings of Israel, with the result that the danger from the Syrians was outwitted and avoided. The Syrian king, told by his captains that Elisha was the shrewd adviser, determined to capture him, and surrounded the hill town of Dothan where the prophet was said to be. In the morning, when Elisha's young servant discovered the surrounding troops, he reported his alarm to his master, to be told, "Fear not, for those who are with us are more than those who are with them." Elisha then prayed that the Lord would open the eyes of his young attendant. His prayer was answered, and he saw that "the mountain was full of chariots of fire round about Elisha!" (2 Kings 6:8-17). The hosts of God were no longer as hostile troops, but as guardian angels protecting God's obedient servants. The restoration of sight was made a general activity of Jesus in his answer to John the Baptiser, who was imprisoned by Herod, but seemed to have had doubts about whether Jesus was the expected one. "Go and tell John what you hear and see," was the instruction of Jesus to John's messengers; "the blind receive their sight and the lame walk, lepers are cleansed and the deaf hear, and the dead are raised up, and the poor have good news preached to them" (Matthew 11:4-5). Our spiritual eyes need to be opened, that we may see into the spiritual order, and become aware of the constant activities of God.

Anyone who has enrolled himself as a disciple of Jesus will want to study the Gospels to discover his teaching about prayer. In the Sermon on the Mount we are told, "When you pray, go into your room and shut the door and pray to your Father who is in secret; and your Father who sees in secret will reward you." The room is not the material one with four walls and a door, but it is the quiet one in the depth of the heart (Matthew 6:6).

Later, the only Gentile writer in the New Testament tells us that on one occasion the disciples found Jesus praying and when he had finished they asked him, "Lord, teach us to pray." In response to this request he gave them the Lord's Prayer, in which we pray first of all for God Himself, that all may know him and revere Him, that his rule may be extended over all, and that his will, so right and good and loving, may be done on earth, as it is by angels, prophets and saints in heaven. Then we are to pray for the things we need for the doing of that holy will – food for the body and soul, forgiveness for the failures and sins of the past, and help to forgive others who sin against us, protection in temptation and deliverance from evil. The first two words of that universal prayer are perhaps the most important, for they express our faith in and our filial relation to Him. They are so full of meaning, that if we got no further than these two opening words, our hearts would be warm with the thought of his loving relationship with us, especially if we use his own loving familiar word, *Abba*. The last words of that great prayer express the worship with which we began: "For thine is the Kingdom, the Power and the Glory, for ever and ever", the final word denoting our agreement with all that precedes it: Amen. So be it!

As I look back to my inner training in prayer, I see an early stage when it consisted of asking God's blessing on myself and those I loved, then through a stage of mental meditation, and finally a merging into contemplation, which did not need words, but a silent awareness of the presence of God, which sometimes continued for a quarter of an hour or more.

When the Second World War broke out in Europe, it was difficult to get supplies of helpful books, and when the Japanese came into it after the disaster of Pearl Harbour, I myself, as well as the clergy and students for whom I had a pastoral responsibility, felt the need of prayers to meet the threatening danger, as well as the provision of prayers which would express a Christ-like spirit about war, enemies in war, dangers in war and sufferers in war. I tried to meet this personal and pastoral need in a four-page leaflet with printed prayers for the occasions mentioned above. That was the beginning of a series of small books of prayers spread over the next fifty years, which were prayed first and then made available for others who felt the same spiritual need as myself.

From that small beginning I noted down quotations that I found meaningful, prayers that I found helpful to my spiritual life, occasionally writing a prayer that almost wrote itself after a meditation. That continued with some effort for the next twenty-five years, when I had the good fortune to be introduced to Lady Collins, who had inspired a succession of what was eventually called Fount Books, some reprints of more expensive books, some specially written for her series, both varieties being published in paperback, at the lowest possible price. Our friendship developed and she invited me to write a Fount book. Pondering on her invitation, suddenly the idea came to me that my collection of quotations and prayers could form the basis of a helpful book, and in a short time an anthology took shape under the title of *Journey for a Soul*. It was finally accepted during the 1973 war between Israel and the surrounding Arab nations. In the sixteen years since, it has sold 75,000 copies, and people are still finding it helpful, and I myself often take a chapter for meditation, when my own spirit feels low and dry.

There had been several small books published earlier. Among them was *In His Name*, which was put together in response to the need expressed by the Conference of the International Missionary Council held at Willengen in Germany in 1952, for a book which would help missionary-minded Christians pray for the Church and the World in a way integrated in the full range of Christian faith and worship.

In my five years in Jerusalem, I used to spend two early hours each day in the private chapel of Bishop's House. From this devotional discipline there developed a book of prayers from the many duties of an archbiship in that troubled area, which SPCK published in a beautiful form with the title of *Jerusalem Prayers for the World Today*. The opening prayer was one prayed by a Muslim woman who lived in Jerusalem around the year AD 800. Rabia's prayer has been a most inspiring one to me, living in Jerusalem 1100 years after she did. I learnt it by heart and pray it often:

O my God,
  if I worship thee in desire for heaven,
    exclude me from heaven;
  If I worship thee for fear of hell,
    burn me in hell.
  But if I worship thee for thyself alone,
    then withhold not from me thine eternal beauty.

That prayer, convinced me, if I needed convincing, that God was active among people of other faiths and traditions than my own.

Since retiring in 1973, I have been able to continue my early morning devotion, from which has emerged every six months a small book of personal prayers or musings about prayer. One such little book was the *Practice of Prayer*. Another, which I value highly and use almost daily, was *Understanding the Psalms*, which gained much from the Jewish commentary on the Psalms by Rabbi

A. Cohen, published by the Soncino Press in 1945. Both of these small books are published by Mowbrays of Oxford.

There is one other book which I must mention in this survey which is in danger of becoming a self-advertising catalogue. This is *The Oxford Book of Prayer*. Soon after my retirement the Oxford University Press approached me with the suggestion that I might collect and edit an anthology of prayers. I did not feel capable of doing this adequately, so I suggested that they should approach Mother Jane of the Sisters of the Love of God at Fairacres in east Oxford. She replied that she and her community would co-operate in this task on one condition, namely that I should be the General Editor. My response was to make one condition of my own – that the anthology should include prayers from other religions. This was willingly accepted by Mother Jane and the Oxford University Press. So began eight years of happy fellowship, under an editorial committee of six members. The book was finished in 1985, and in the first year 30,000 copies of the hardback edition were sold; later a paperback was published, and still further *The Pocket Oxford Book of Prayer*, in an attractive and durable format, for long life with regular use. The prices fixed by OUP were extremely reasonable. The members of the editorial group spontaneously agreed that the royalties should be devoted to spiritual and charitable purposes.

During that eight years' task, those at the heart of it were learning themselves how to pray more deeply and contemplatively. I myself was greatly encouraged and inspired by Eric Milner-White, Dean of York and before that Dean of King's College, Cambridge. His early books were *Daily Prayer*, compiled jointly with Canon G.W. Briggs of Worcester in 1941, and *After the Third Collect*. The book of his that still nourishes my inner spirit is *My God My Glory*, published by SPCK in 1954. His *Procession of Passion Prayers* gives welcome prayers for devotion in meditation on our Lord's revelation of God's eternal love. The following prayers have inspired me more than any comments can adequately express my gratitude:

Help Me to Pray –

My God and Father
  help me to pray
    as my first work,
    my unremitting work,
    my highest, finest, and dearest work;
  As the work I do for Thee, and by Thee,
    and with Thee,
    for thy other children and
    for the whole world.
Let my prayer be a channel for your love, your grace,
    your peace for those for whom I pray, and for
    myself, O dear and blessed Lord.

Right Choice –

Lord, in the choices of every day,
  Grant me to choose aright
    as in thy Presence and to thy glory:
  to discriminate not only
    between the good and the evil,
    but between the good and the better,
    and to do the best.

Before Bible Study –

Convey to me, O Holy Spirit,
    through the familiar phrases, fresh understanding;
    through passages passed over or unapprehended,
      new treasure;
    through thy grace – insight, conviction, guidance,
    revelation, glory.

Crucified with Christ

O God our Father, help us to nail to the Cross of
thy dear Son our selfish nature,
the wrong desires of the heart,
the sinful devisings of the mind,

51

the corrupt apprehensions of the eyes,
the cruel words of the tongue,
the ill employment of hands and feet;
that the old man being crucified and done away,
the new man may live and grow
in the glorious likeness of the
same thy Son Jesus Christ;
Who liveth and reigneth
with Thee and the Holy Ghost,
one God, world without end.

In addition to that great teacher of prayer, there were others to whom I owe a debt of gratitude. Among them is Boethius (480-524), whose lovely prayer I regularly use;

O Father, give the spirit power to climb
To the fountain of all light, and be purified.
Break through the mists of earth, the weight of the clod,
Shine forth in splendour, Thou that art calm weather,
And quiet resting place for faithful souls.
To see Thee is the end and the beginning,
Thou carriest us, and Thou dost go before,
Thou art the journey, and the journey's end.

Another is Alcuin (735-804), who was called from York by the Emperor Charlemagne to be head of his Palace School. In a letter written shortly before his death to his friend Adelhard, Archbishop of Canterbury, he foresees that day and requests his old friend:

That day, remember me, and say:
  "O Christ most gentle,
  Have mercy on a poor man, Alcuin."
And now,
Beside the shore of the sail-winged sea
I wait the coming of God's silent dawn.

Do thou help this my journey with thy prayer.
I ask this, with a devoted heart.

I cannot forget the visits I paid to Norwich and sat quietly in
the reconstructed cell of Julian the hermitess of Norwich, meditating on the *Sixteen Shewings of Divine Love* which she received in
May 1373. This is the first book known to have been written by
a woman in English, and is recognised as one of the great spiritual
writings. One of the passages that I can never forget says

> He showed me a little thing, the size of a hazelnut, in the
> palm of my hand, and it was as round as a ball. I looked at
> it with my mind's eye and I thought, "What can this be?"
> And answer came, "It is all that is made." I marvelled that
> it could last, for I thought it might have crumbled to nothing,
> it was so small. And the answer came into my mind, "It lasts
> and ever shall because God loves it." And all things have
> being through the love of God. In this little thing I saw three
> truths. The first is God made it. The second is God loves it.
> The third is that God looks after it.

About pain, trouble and distress, Julian says another unforgettable
thing:

> He did not say, "You shall not be tempest-tossed, You shall
> not be work-weary, you shall not be discomforted." But he
> said, "You shall not be overcome."

Julian urges us, "Every morning put your mind into your heart
and stand in the presence of God all the day long." She insists
that we should see God primarily as all loving, and claims that
"Love is his meaning" and that we are all enfolded in that love.

Another writer of the fourteenth century who has helped my
spiritual life is the anonymous author of the *Cloud of Unknowing*,
another early devotional book in English. He teaches that all
thoughts, all concepts, all images must be buried beneath a cloud

of forgetting, while our love divested of thought must rise toward God, hidden in a cloud of unknowing: "He is not to be gotten or holden by thought but only by love."

A longer quotation speaks of the cloud between God and the praying soul:

For at the first time thou findest but a darkness and, as it were, a cloud of unknowing, thou knowest not what, save that thou feelest in thy will a naked intent unto God. This darkness and this cloud is betwixt thee and thy God, and telleth thee that thou mayest neither see him clearly by light of understanding, nor feel him in sweetness of love in thine affection, and therefore shape thee to bide in this darkness as long as thou mayest, crying after him that thou lovest . . . Then he will sometimes peradventure send a beam of ghostly light piercing this cloud of unknowing that is betwixt thee and him, and show thee some of his privity of the which man may not nor cannot speak.

The same mystical author wrote another treatise entitled *The Epistle of Privy Counsel*, in which he speaks more simply;

That I am and how that I am, as in nature and in grace, all I have it of thee, Lord, and thou it art. And all I offer it unto thee, principally to the praising of thee, for the help of all mine even Christians and of me.

There are others in the six hundred years between us today and Julian and our unidentified author of *The Cloud*. I must limit myself to two others who have thrilled and inspired me.

The first is George MacDonald (1824-1905). He was educated at Aberdeen University. He became a Congregational minister, but his views about God's inclusive care for the "heathen" and his views about the divine revelation in the Bible, brought him into conflict with the narrow-mindedness of some of his congregation, and in 1893 he left the ministry to devote himself to writing.

My interest in MacDonald began when I was given a well-worn copy of his *Unspoken Sermons*. I managed to secure all three volumes and also a copy of the *Miracles of our Lord*, and learnt much about prayer, and trust in God. I was grateful for C.S. Lewis's *George MacDonald Anthology*, in which he declared that his conversion to Christianity was humanly due to the posthumous influence of MacDonald. His series of short, pithy quotations, mainly from the *Unspoken Sermons*, stimulated my heart and mind.

George MacDonald was a friend of John Ruskin, Lewis Carroll, Charles Kingsley, F.D. Maurice, and many others. He wrote a whole series of novels in which the characters personified some of his leading insights. He said that he took to writing novels to support himself and his family and to enable him to devote himself to his religious writings and poems. C.S. Lewis followed MacDonald in writing imaginative and mythical stories about the spiritual life. If any readers want to learn more about MacDonald, I would urge them to read William Raeper's splendid biography of the great Victorian visionary, published as recently as 1987, and now in a paperback edition. It will be a great happiness to meet George MacDonald in eternity, if I get there as well.

The other writer who has deeply interested me is Jan Struther, the Mrs Miniver of the Second World War. I first came across her in a marriage hymn in *Songs of Praise*, which I still feel is the best that has ever been composed for a Christian wedding. The first verse gives one the feeling of the whole poem:

God, whose eternal mind
　Rules the round world over,
Whose wisdom lies behind
　All that men discover:
Grant that we, by thought and speech,
May grow nearer each to each:
　Lord, let sweet converse bind
　　Lover unto lover,
　　　Bless us, God of loving.

A morning hymn, sometimes used in Advent, sings:

> High o'er the lonely hills
>   Black turns to grey,
> Birdsong the valley fills,
>   Mists fold away;
> Grey wakes to green again,
> Beauty is seen again –
> Gold and serene again
>   Dawneth the day.
>
> So, o'er the hills of life,
>   Stormy, forlorn,
> Out of the cloud and strife
>   Sunrise is born;
> Swift grows the light for us;
> Ended is night for us;
> Soundless and bright for us
>   Breaketh God's morn.

All the twelve hymns included in *Songs of Praise* could be happily quoted, if time and space allowed. I must content myself with the last verse of a hymn in honour of St Bartholomew:

> Time, take our words and do what thou wilt with them;
> Death, take our hands and all that we built with them;
> Only our faith, our soul's endeavour,
> Take it, Lord, make it, Lord, shine for ever.

There are some recent lessons that I have learnt about prayer, and meditation. I have become aware of three stages, all three of which deserve equal attention and time spent on them. They are preparation, actual prayer either vocal or silent, and listening to God.

In the first, we detach ourselves from our preoccupations, even our plans for his service, quieten our minds and fix our attention on God, lifting our hearts in hope, trust, and love.

In the second, we thank God for all that He is and does, especially for his revelation in Jesus Christ. Then we bring before Him our needs, hold before Him those whom we love and for whom we have a concern. We may pour out our hearts about the situation in which we find ourselves, expressing our trust, hope and confidence.

Finally, we open mind and heart, so that He may shed his light on our path, and tell us anything that He wants us to do. I find often that nothing clear and definite comes until sometime later, possibly on the next morning, sometimes when carrying out the seemingly pedestrian duties of the day, when a short, crystallised thought comes into the mind with clarity and authority. It isn't that God delays his guidance and message, but that our perception takes time to put it into words.

Another insight that has been coming to me consistently is that instead of beseeching God to undertake certain actions or to grant certain mercies or blessings we should state our faith that He is already and always at work in the way that we desire, so that our petition becomes an expansion of our address to Him, a relative clause expressing our conviction of faith that He is already doing what we were about to request Him to do. Thus, "O God, You are always more ready to hear than we are to pray"; or, "O God, You are preparing for those who love You, such good things as pass man's understanding, You pour into our hearts such love toward You, and help us to love You above all things, and give us your promises which exceed all that we desire."

Alongside this, I have to remember the teaching of Jesus, "Ask, and it will be given you, seek and you will find, knock and it will be opened to you." It is as if we have to be deeply conscious of our need and eager for God's promised blessings.

So far, I have thought mainly in terms of our personal relationship with God. I have also to think of how our prayers may be helpful to God, especially in regard to desperate situations in the world. My hope is that by praying about such situations I am helping to keep God from being pushed out, forgotten or ignored.

The second clue is that most man-made tragedies arise from wrong attitudes within the minds and wills of people. So the struggle is basically a spiritual one. Our wrestling, as St Paul reminds us, is not against human foes, but against cosmic powers, against organisations and powers in the spiritual milieu.

The psychologist Jung believed that there is a common unconscious in which we are all included and so able to influence the psychic dimension in some degree. I often think that our sociological relationships are like an action in which each person is a small knot so that we can influence the common situation in four directions.

Further, as we link these seemingly hopeless situations to God in prayer, he will help us to see hidden possibilities within them. I must never forget that He can influence us to right interpretation and thinking and even to some inspired initiative of love.

A very last thought is that we must do everything possible to answer our own prayers. Not all that happens is God's will. There are situations for which we humans are responsible, either by neglect or corporate selfishness. We need penitence for these, and a determination to set them right, and above all the confident belief that God is always at work to bring blessing out of everything, however seemingly tragic and hopeless:

All manner of thing shall be well.

CHAPTER 7

The War Comes to Burma

C hristmas Day 1941 saw a bad air-raid on Rangoon in which many were killed and injured. A party of Holy Cross students and I went to the Dufferin Hospital, most of whose nurses had fled. We washed the blood-stained floors, while my wife and other missionary workers helped in the wards and the laundry.

As the fear of raids increased, I became an ambulance driver, on duty mainly through the nights, while women drivers took the day shifts. Fortunately there were never again as many casualties, so our service consisted mainly in standing by.

Japanese troops moved into Burma from Thailand and Malaya and advanced threateningly on Rangoon, so on 30th January 1942 my wife and three children left the city on a crowded river steamer, to go north to Mandalay and from there on by road to Maymyo. On the journey our eldest child picked up bubonic plague, and when the steamer moored at Chauk my wife managed to get medicines from the BOC Hospital shortly before it closed.

With the fall of Singapore the fate of Rangoon seemed sealed and on 19th February I paid my last visit to the Delta, to bring back our missionary nurse and to confer with village clergy and elders and teachers about what should be done if the worst happened. The scene will always live in my memory. We were squatting cross-legged on the floor of the mission house at Nyaung-ngu, half a dozen priests and a dozen men and women teachers. The first question to be settled was what the missionaries should do. I explained that we men were ready to stay if the meeting felt it was right for us to do so. Ma Pwa Sein, the stalwart headmistress of St Mary's, Kemmendine, which had transferred to the Delta at the outbreak of war, was very emphatic that we should not fall into the hands of the Japanese. Another speaker said that our presence would only draw attention and suspicion to their villages. The tension was relieved by Own Bwint, our senior Karen priest. With a kindly and humorous look at me he said, "Well, we could dress you in Burmese clothes, we could darken your skin and dye your hair. You speak Burmese well enough. But we could do nothing with that English nose of yours."

The meeting decided that the missionaries should move to Upper Burma, for at that time we fully believed the government's assurance that we should be able to hold part of Burma at any rate. So that evening Sister Websper and I, with a dozen or more girl students, scrambled on board an already crowded steamer, which waited in mid-stream while we pulled out to it in sampans and canoes. Neither we, nor the shadowy crowds on the bank calling out blessings and affectionate greetings, realised that it was a last farewell, though we had misgivings. Yet it was so, for when we docked at Rangoon next morning civil evacuation had been ordered, to be completed within forty-eight hours, and the wharves were black with excited refugees, who insisted on crowding on to the boat before we could get off.

I spent the rest of 20th February, which happened to be my fortieth birthday, taking the girl students back to their homes in and around Rangoon. The next day I went to see the military commander to ask for permission to stay on to look after stray people and perhaps give pastoral care to the officials and troops left in the city. He refused, so after a visit to the General Hospital, almost empty of patients and deserted by Burmese staff, with the remaining civilian doctors and sisters about to leave, I set off sadly with several stragglers and drove through the night to Prome.

At Prome my car, a rather seedy second-hand one, broke its big end. No spare parts were available but a small bus-load of Indian servants from our diocesan girls' school in Rangoon picked me up and took me on with them. At Pyinmana I called on

Brayton Case, the gallant Baptist agricultural missionary who had for twenty years organised a training farm. He was feeling critical about a number of his American missionary colleagues who weeks earlier had left their posts to obey the early warnings of the US Embassy to leave Burma.

A heart-warming incident took place at a little up-country town where we rested to get a midday meal. I went into what seemed to me a Burmese restaurant. The hostess came to greet me, and in reply to my question said that chicken curry was cooking, which I ordered with satisfaction. After making a good meal I asked how much I owed.

"Nothing," was the reply of the smiling Burmese matron.

"But you can't run a business on these lines."

"That is true," she said, and then with a friendly twinkle, "This isn't a restaurant; it's a private house."

I mention this incident because it is typical of Burmese friendliness and hospitality, and during the retreat many people like myself experienced similar kindliness.

Finally I reached Maymyo, to find my family camping out in a very small house, all three children down with scarlet fever.

In Maymyo I was at first rather at a loose end, for most of the civilian families had left, and the Establishment chaplain was there to carry on the church services and to look after the few people left. So I began to visit the civil hospital which had been taken over by the military for wounded and sick men from the British forces further south. It soon became apparent that men were being discharged too soon, to make room for a growing number of casualties. A convalescent home was needed, so I got permission to use two houses which had been the homes of senior staff of the Bombay Burma Trading Company. These were used to house twenty to twenty-five convalescent officers. For the other ranks we took over St Michael's girls' school which was able to take about seventy men. My wife acted as housekeeper for the officers' houses and Mrs Weaverhurst, the headmistress, took charge of St Michael's.

It was not easy to get the necessary equipment, bedding, etc.,

61

for army regulations did not deal with the issue of such things to an unattached missionary. However, there seemed to be nothing against lending equipment to non-military personnel, and we got most of what was wanted. Lady Dorman-Smith, the wife of the Governor, came to our rescue with two generous gifts of money. Dry and tinned stores were issued readily, but meat, vegetables and fruit were not so easy to procure, and often I went out into the surrounding villages to buy up food which normally would have come into the Maymyo bazaar.

We did our best to keep the men amused with socials and off-the-cuff concerts, but the thing which was most appreciated was the homely atmosphere provided by my wife and three children and by Mrs Weaverhurst and a few Maymyo friends still left.

As the war moved northwards, there was greater pressure on the hospital and our convalescent homes. Stocks of petrol were low, and late one afternoon cars passing the orderly room were stopped by an irate major-general, who berated us for using valuable petrol at such a time of crisis. Approaching the car I was driving, he reproved me, saying that a padre ought to know better. I replied somewhat heatedly that I was more or less on duty, visiting men in the hospital. He then asked my name, and on hearing it, asked if I was the padre at the convalescent homes, adding, "A damned fine job. Pass, friend!"

The war came nearer and my family went with the last train out of Maymyo, with hundreds of Anglo-Burman mothers and children proceeding northwards to Shwebo or Myitkyina for air evacuation to Assam. Domestic help grew more difficult, but things were eased by the arrival of the Reverend George Tidey, another SPG missionary. There was no water-borne sanitation, and every other day Tidey and I had to empty the few sanitary buckets, burying their contents in holes dug in the garden, as well as trying to keep the houses clean and collecting fruit and vegetables.

It was clear that our troops would not be able to hold out much longer, so we got most of the convalescent men away, making for

Mohnyin where there was a small hospital organised by the Bible Churchmen's Missionary Society. That was on Saturday, 25th April. Two sergeants and I stayed behind to try to salvage as much as we could of our stores of food.

The next day Professor Pearn, who was working in intelligence, came in to warn me that the Japs were breaking through from Taung-gyi and that it was only a matter of hours before they would reach Maymyo. I think it was on that Sunday, but it may have been on the Sunday before, that I gave the last message from the Burma Broadcasting Service. The Indian in charge of it had to do all the technical work himself, and I gave the short address that had been scheduled. I remember saying that there were dangerous days ahead which would call for faithfulness and courage, quoting the text from the Psalms: "He will not be afraid of any evil tidings, for his heart standeth fast in the Lord." I said that one day we should be back, and that in the meantime our affection for the people of Burma would not fail. I have never met anyone who heard that broadcast, but the Indian superintendent and I felt we had seen the job through to the end.

As soon as I had finished speaking, the small emergency wireless station was dismantled, and I rushed back to my two sergeants to get ready to leave. At nine o'clock that night we set out in the pouring rain, our car packed with people and stores of food, picking our way through lorries, mules and men on foot. By the time we reached the Ava Bridge it had stopped raining and having got across, we just lay on the ground and got a few hours' sleep.

Refreshed, we drove on to Shwebo and had breakfast with a small group of SPG missionaries who had camped out there, looking after the stream of refugees hoping to be flown to India. The airlift had now stopped and people were being moved on to Myitkyina, hoping to get a plane there. In the hospital was the Reverend E.C. Turner from St Michael's Mission to the Blind, who had been attacked by dacoits a few days earlier and left for dead a few miles out of Shwebo. For several days he was at death's door, and a grave had been kept ready in case the worst happened. He was making a wonderful recovery and in the few hours we were there we managed to get him on to an ambulance train – off to Myitkyina to be flown out to India.

We motored on a further thirty miles and when the road ended were lucky to get on a goods train with our precious stock of food. At Naba we were overtaken by the hospital train and discovered that their food supply had run out, so we handed over a whole case of sausages and one of tinned peaches. I also heard that a party of girls from Bishop's Home orphanage school in Rangoon had got stranded at Katha and I was able to send a telegram to Jack Cardew of the Burma Railways asking him to extricate them and get them on a train to Myitkyina.

At Mohnyin ten convalescent officers and twenty-eight men, the two faithful sergeants and myself got off the hospital train and made for the hospital of the BCMS where Dr Russell and the two nursing sisters took us all in and gave medical treatment to those needing it. Food was short and for two days I was kept running round trying to buy up supplies, with the result that I had to retire to bed with blistered feet. The next morning orders came through that the able-bodied were to begin the trek to India and the rest get to Myitkyina to take the chance of a plane. Dr Russell insisted that I went with the convalescent men and we were lucky to pick up one of the last trains to go northwards. At one station we were stopped for several hours alongside a troop train on which I discovered the Reverend R.H.L. Slater, now enrolled as an army chaplain, who told me the comforting news that my wife and three children had got away from Myitkyina a day or two earlier. This was the first news I had had of them since they had left Maymyo a fortnight earlier.

At Myitkyina we camped out for the night in a mission schoolroom and early next morning managed to get a lift out to the airstrip two miles away. The rough emergency airfield was crowded with several hundred people, mainly women and children, and in the whole day only two planes came in, dropped some cases of food, took on wounded and as many women and children as they could pack in, and were quickly off again.

Towards nightfall most of the refugees went back into Myitkyina for the night, but the remaining convalescents and I were
too tired to do this, so we stayed on the airfield. The men asked
my permission to open a case of tea and a case of tins of sausages
from the stores brought by the two planes. I had no authority to
do this, but agreed that it was a sensible thing to do. No sooner
had we done so when a staff officer drove up in a car, accused
us of looting and ordered us to put the tins back in the cases. We
did so, obediently, waited for an hour, then took them out again,
made a fire out of the cases and ate one of the most welcome
meals I have ever enjoyed – of tea and hot sausages. Then we
wrapped ourselves in every bit of clothing we could find and lay
down on the ground to get some sleep.

At dawn next morning two Chinese planes came in and we got
almost everyone on board and away. Only half a dozen men and
I were left, but almost at once a third plane arrived, and having
been warned that they dared not wait as there were Jap planes
about, we got on board and the plane took off almost empty. I
have never felt so unhappy in my life as I did on that short airlift
to Dibrugarh, leaving Burma almost entirely in the hands of the
Japanese, and knowing how many hundreds of people were
stranded on the railway line below Myitkyina. A fourth plane
came in at Dibrugarh while we were waiting there, and that was
the last. The next day the Japs bombed the Myitkyina airfield and
air evacuation ceased.

Reflecting afterwards on that short first Burma campaign,
several things came to my mind:

Most of us civilians accepted the official assurances that some
part of Burma would be held, and so we stayed put. We should
have known that once Singapore fell there was little hope of
holding Burma.

The Japanese had been trained in jungle warfare, and knew
how to trek across country and live on the jungle. Our troops
could only move on the roads and had to be supplied with food.

I could not help feeling proud of the missionary personnel who
had done so much to help the fleeing refugees at Shwebo,

Mohnyin and Myitkyina, and elsewhere. And I remembered our faithful Christians – Burmese, Karen, Chin and others – left on their own, with the certainty of being suspected as friends of the British and Americans, their hearts heavy with fear about our safety.

The Burmese people had been quietly loyal and kind. There was little or no sabotage behind the lines. Burmese women were at the railway stations with food, fruit and water for the refugees on the crowded trains.

General Alexander and his troops carried out a magnificent fighting retreat and held up the Japanese advance until the rains broke, thus saving four months' valuable time in which preparations could be made to repel the Japs if they attempted to invade India.

Dibrugarh was crowded with refugees. British, Anglo-Indians and Indians did a splendid job in receiving us. Beds were provided in churches and halls, two meals a day were available for all of us. Slowly we made our way by steamer and train down to Calcutta, to join our families and wonder about the future.

In India we missionaries were at a loose end. Military and government people were quickly absorbed into the war effort, but the churches were at a loss what to do with us. My wife and I went to Poona and for nine months took charge of the Willingdon Soldiers' Club, at a time when welfare and amenities work was only just beginning. At the end of that period, in May 1943, Hugh Wilson, who was in charge of the Rangoon diocese, Bishop West being in the USA recovering from a severe motor accident, agreed that we should move to Simla so that I might maintain liaison with the Burma Government-in-exile that had made its headquarters there.

CHAPTER 8

In Exile

It was a great joy to get back to so many Burma people, government officers from almost all the departments, and a small number of Burmans, including Paw Tun, chairman of the Executive Council, Htun Aung Gyaw, the Finance Member, and three brilliant members of the Indian Civil Service from one family – Tin Tut, Kyaw Min and Kyaw Tha.

B.R. Pearn had been appointed Information Officer, and had already produced a booklet for the Indian Army HQ, compiled with the help of experienced District and Forest Officers, with valuable advice on how to live in the jungle. With the help of departmental officers a Burma Handbook was being compiled, dealing with the country and peoples of Burma, production, communications, a short history, a valuable Who's Who, health notes, and a map with the scale of thirty-two miles to the inch.

Pearn and I were very concerned to ensure that the troops who would liberate Burma should know something of the country and its people, for the army that fought the retreat in 1942 had had little time to learn any of the background. Few of the troops could distinguish easily between Burmans, Chinese and Japanese. The Japanese had been very clever in disguising themselves as Burmans and sometimes as Buddhist monks, with the result that many of the troops looked upon the Burmese as a lot of traitors. Professor Pearn and I had for the last ten years been interchangeably secretary and editor of the Burma Research Society, and when we discovered that the Society's bank had been able to get our balance safely into India before the break-up, we conceived the plan of a series of Burma Pamphlets, describing various aspects of the national life. We were fortunate in finding

Longmans (India) interested in the project, and with the aid of a subsidy for each book were able to put the price as low as eight annas a copy, and in return for the subsidy were able to hand over a sizeable number of each book for distribution to the Army, Navy and RAF. All the authors gave their manuscripts free, to help make Burma and its people better known, not only to the men of the forces, but more widely.

It concerned me deeply that the men going back to Burma should have a smattering of the language, especially those who would go in with the Wingate levies into occupied Burma. So I compiled a booklet entitled *Rubbing Along in Burmese*, adapting the pronunciation as closely as possible to English and dispensing with niceties that involved training in phonetics. I offered the booklet to GHQ, Simla, but after two months had had no reply. So I went in person to enquire what had happened to it, and after several more weeks heard that a first edition of fifty thousand copies was being printed. I never saw any acknowledgement nor received a word of thanks. However, a year or more later I got a note from Colonel Leslie Glass saying that in a report received from an officer dropped behind the Japanese lines there occurred the statement, "I think I ought to add that I owe my life to a little booklet entitled *Rubbing Along in Burmese*."

In the latter part of 1943 I was appointed Archdeacon of Rangoon, in which capacity I was enabled to visit groups of Anglo-Burman Anglicans and others who had settled in various Indian centres. I also took part in conferences of Burma missionaries in Lahore, Lucknow and Mussourie, in which we began to think about the revival of our considerable educational work. In a letter to my wife I spoke of a whole-day conference about the future of Judson College, in which I pressed the representatives of the American Baptist Mission to make Judson into an ecumenical college and to be ready to be integrated into a University unitary system. I realised that the standard of scholarship of the staff of Judson was not as high as that of the rest of the University, but their care of the students seemed to me more personal. I was critical of the plans of the Burma Educational Service and government advisers to absorb Judson into the one system, and I hoped that through Judson Western members of staff might be able to continue to serve students when the process of Burmanising the University inevitably took place.

For Christmas 1943 I was asked by Air India to broadcast a Christmas message to Christians in Southeast Asia, which I was glad to do, having our Christian friends of different races in Burma much in mind.

Some time towards the end of 1943 I was approached by the US Office of War Information to see if I would join their staff as adviser on Burmese subjects and language. This office was to move to Assam in preparation for developments planned for the Katha-Naba-Bhamo area. They seemed ready to take me on my own terms, with a Burmese assistant to be selected by myself, a stenographer, a salary four times as big as my missionary stipend, with considerable amenities. The proposal sounded attractive and I was eager to get into any part of Burma. But enquiries from two missionary friends already recruited as Kachin advisers made me realise that there would be little opportunity to influence policy and relationships. Everything would be geared to quite ruthless war operations. So, being more concerned for understanding relationships with the Burmese, I declined the USOWI offer.

While *Rubbing Along in Burmese* was being printed, I was working on a bigger handbook for learning the language, under the title of *Three Months' Hard Labour*. This followed the technique of the book which had helped me most in my early years – R. Grant Brown's *Half the Battle in Burmese*. The Roman script was phonetic and the book consisted of a series of dialogues, building up with phrases rather than individual words. Only in the final chapter was the transference made to Burmese script. The book was printed at the Jubbulpore Mission Press where the Reverend L.A. Crain of the ABM Press of Rangoon was superintending Burmese printing. The publication was subsidised by the Burma Government-in-exile. I had at one time abandoned hope that the little book would ever be published, for the only copy, typed laboriously by myself, was stolen from a railway carriage on Delhi

Station. However, an extra month's hard labour made good the loss.

At the same time I was working on a small English-Burmese dictionary with about 3,500 of the most common words likely to be needed by government workers going back into Burma when liberation should come. This was the only one of the three language efforts for which I received any payment; in this case an honorarium from the Burma Government of thirty pounds.

In the latter half of 1943 George West, Bishop of Rangoon, got back from the USA. Shortly after his arrival he got together a conference of Anglo-Burmans, who agreed that when they returned to Burma they would ally themselves more closely with the people of the country rather than as exclusively with the British side of their heritage as they had tended to do in pre-war days. George Kirkham sent out an appeal to all Anglo-Burman Associations asking their members to go back to Burma in this spirit, and demanding no special safeguards.

In early 1944 I was asked by the Burma Government if I would consider deputising for B.R. Pearn while he went on a much-needed furlough. I was glad to do this, for I had kept in close touch with his work and took a deep interest in it. It was an interesting time to be at the centre, for news was beginning to get through from Burma and plans for reconstruction after liberation were being drawn up.

In February 1943 Wingate had made his first long-range penetration into North Burma, cut the railway in seventy places and crossed the Irrawaddy. These raiders maintained contact with their base by wireless, and were supplied by air. Their guides and interpreters were Anglo-Burmans, Karens, Kachins and Burmans. They were splendidly received by the villagers wherever they went, although the Japanese took brutal revenge afterwards on all who had welcomed them. This expedition, in addition to proving a new method of jungle warfare, did another great thing for British troops: it convinced them of the friendliness of the people of Burma, for many of them who had fought through the 1942 campaign had prejudiced memories of those hard days. In this first Wingate expedition many Christian Karens took part. Bernard Fergusson, who was in charge of one of Wingate's columns, pays this tribute to them in his epic account, *Beyond the Chindwin*:

> These men form the bulk of the Burma Rifles, and my platoon consisted entirely of them . . . Nobody who has served with Karens could fail to like them. Thoroughly biddable, and mostly Christian (to a degree which would put to shame most people who profess and call themselves such), they make admirable soldiers – intelligent, willing, energetic, brave . . . Billy, the Havildar-Major, was a tiny, wizened man, always smiling and very devout, who never went to sleep without first singing softly to himself all three verses of "Jesus loves me, this I know". He was a particular favourite among the British troops.

The early months of 1944 saw two further Allied successes. In February the Japanese made a great effort to surround a British and Indian force in Arakan, but the result was a resounding victory for our men, who had indeed been cut off for some days, but supplied by air. Fighting with tremendous courage, they turned the tables completely. Meanwhile, General Stilwell advanced up the Hukawng Valley with American-trained Chinese troops. To aid him, a large airborne force of Chindits was landed on the wide bend of the Irrawaddy between Bhamo and Katha. Two SPG men accompanied this force as chaplains – David Patterson and John Matthew. Unfortunately David was killed when his glider made a crash-landing. He had served since the outbreak of the war with Japan. His quiet friendliness, calm courage and sense of humour endeared him to all, Burmans and British alike. His death was a great loss. In a letter written just before this last trip he asked the Bishop to act as his next-of-kin, mentioned a small legacy to the diocese, and added that he hoped to benefit the Church in Burma with many years of service rather than with a paltry sum of money.

Large parts of Upper Burma began to be liberated, including mission districts of the BCMS. Bill Crittle, the Field Secretary, was able to visit the Kamaing-Mogaung area in his capacity as a worker of the USOWI. He found that Christians had stood firmly by their faith and practice; only one family had lapsed, and that had been very weak, even in the best of times. Christians had been compelled to give up meetings for corporate worship, but still kept up small prayer meetings in houses. The care with which Christians had treasured their Bibles, prayer books and hymn books was very touching.

Military chaplains moved in with the troops, and news of the Christian community came to us through them. Letters from one of them told of Mohnyin, another BCMS centre, where the nurses from the Mandalay Children's Hospital had settled. One of these had married an Indian Christian doctor, and together they worked for the sick and wounded, although badly handicapped by the lack of medicines. In a nearby village girls of the Mission to the Blind had been settled before the final evacuation; they continued with their weaving, and a recent army photograph showed them at work at their looms, surrounded by admiring soldiers and villagers.

About this time Brayton Case, the American Baptist missionary, lost his life. He had been touring in the liberated areas trying to get agriculture going again. Proceeding up a flooded stream flowing into the Indaw-gyi Lake with a heavy load of paddy (rice) seed, the boat capsized and Case was thrown into the water and drowned. He had lived most of his sixty years in Burma, being the son of missionary parents. He built up the Agricultural Training School of Pyinmana, spoke Burmese like a Burman, and was an out-and-out evangelist. One was always conscious of him as a great Christian; only later did you become conscious of his denominational affiliation.

Pearn and the members of his staff had started a monthly publication called *Burma Today*, giving news brought out by men who had gone in with Wingate, photographs taken by army photographers or by RAF planes on patrol, and first-hand accounts by people smuggled out of occupied Burma or coming out from the growing number of liberated areas. This was naturally continued and copies were distributed all over India, sent to all publicity agencies and taken into Burma. It made people conscious that we were in touch with our friends in Burma again and it generated a spirit of confidence that liberation was only a matter of time. In one of the monthly issues I tried to express the affection of British government officers, missionaries, and commercial people for the country in which they had worked and to which they longed to return. It was as follows:

A Briton Speaks
(Lines written in exile in 1944)

"It is
As I suppose
The fairest place
In all the earth."[1]
So told
That Briton first
Who visited
This Burma and appraised her worth.

Pagan . . .
Where Burman Kings
The desert made
Flower to beauty,
Buddha's
Peace enshrining,
Age of greatness
Given to spirit, teaching five-fold duty.

Ploughing . . .
Fields of water,
Women planting
Laughing voices.
Reaping . . .

Rustling paddy,
Wind-touched music,
Bounteous harvest, Burma's heart rejoices.

Smiling
Happy faces,
Nor proud nor fearing,
Equal brothers.
No itch
For wealth or greed
Contanted if
$Wun\text{-}sa^2$ sufficient for life's need.

But now
At hostile word
Those friends of old
Learning to hate!
Those friends
Who underneath
Shy outer shell
Would labour still to make her great.

1 Ralph Fitch in 1586
2 Wun-sa – literally "food for the stomach", food supply

Together with other departments, the Department of Public relations, as the Information Office was now called, was asked to submit its plans for reconstruction when we should get to Burma. We were warned by the Governor and senior officers of Government not to be extravagant, but to say what we thought would be needed to do an efficient job. Our link with Civil Affairs Service (Burma) in Delhi was Colonel Leslie Glass, and plans were so laid that when the civil government took over from the military, there should be an easy transition from the initial operation under the military.

A broadcasting station would be necessary, with as many radio sets as could be provided; film units to tour the towns and villages; a news service for the newspapers in Burmese and English being

74

published in Rangoon; a daily newspaper in English and a weekly
one in Burmese to give reliable news and print government
communications; and a network of public relations officers at the
headquarters towns of District Commissioners.

Equipment for these services and staff had to be worked out
and costed. In the Department of Public Relations we were
fortunate to have the temporary services of U Kyaw Tha of the
Burma Civil Service to undertake all this planning. He was a most
able officer, and I was able to hand over this part of the work to
him with confidence, while I concentrated on the current activities
of the department.

I was happy in the work because of the acceptance by the
government of my own interpretation of the task of public
relations, namely not to be a propagandist agency acting on the
assumption that the government was always infallibly right; not
only to be an information service about government policies, plans
and activities; but to be an agency interpreting the government
to the people, and feeding back to the government the reactions
and feelings of the people.

I was not a trained publicity man, nor had I any professional
competence in publicity media, and I felt the need of competent
advice from someone expert in this field. We were fortunate in
getting as a consultant Fred Spence, who was the advertising
manager in Calcutta of the Imperial Tobacco Company. Both in
India and after our return to Burma his expert help was invaluable.

Newspaper correspondents and representatives of the Ministry
of Information were frequent visitors to Burma, and we did our
best to give them what news we had, to tell them about
government hopes and plans, and to extract from them any news
and wisdom they had to give us. One interesting visitor was a
man with whom I had a long and interesting talk. Towards the
end of our conversation he asked me what use I would make of
documented evidence that the Japs in Burma had a far-reaching
plan to destroy the Buddhist system of monasteries and monks.
Before the war it was estimated that there were 100,000 monks

in Burma, supposedly concentrating on religious duties and doing no menial work in their monasteries but relying on daily gifts of food from the faithful. Any threat to this monastic system would clearly be material for damaging propaganda. My reply was that I doubted if any such plan had a remote chance of success, and that I would want to be assured of the truthfulness and authenticity of the document he was planning to send me. The argument became heated when I refused to agree that it did not matter if the document was authentic or not. Afterwards he complained bitterly to other government officers of the uselessness of such a DPR, and on being told of my background, retorted angrily, "Why didn't somebody warn me that the man was a bloody missionary?"

Some time during late 1942 an active young Communist named Thein Pe was smuggled out of Burma. He and his friends had collaborated with the Japs, but had quickly seen that the independence granted to Burma was fictitious and that the Burmese people were being exploited for Japanese imperialism. He wrote a short book entitled *What Happened in Burma*, described on the cover as "the frank revelations of a young Burmese revolutionary leader who has recently escaped from Burma to India". Edgar Snow, in a review of it, said, "Here is a young man with a message which ought to be read by every Indian who hopes to see his country free. To achieve its maximum purgative effects, it ought to be digested by every intelligent Englishman who wants to win the war . . . Reading Thein Pe's eye-witness account of what has happened in Burma makes it apparent to any still in doubt that Japan's slogan of 'Asia for the Asiatics' means in reality 'Asia for Japan'."

At the Governor's request I accompanied Thein Pe on a speaking tour. He made no bones about his own nationalistic aims for Burma, but he kept faithfully to his brief and certainly helped Indians to see what would happen if the Japanese were victorious.

I went on tour frequently from Simla to most of the main cities of India, speaking to Indian audiences and getting together groups of refugees from Burma to give them the latest news and to encourage them with hopes of victory and return. I also spoke at various military and RAF centres to tell men in preparation for the invasion of Burma, about the people of the country. At such meetings I was able to commend and distribute copies of the Burma Pamphlets, and also many copies of our information booklet entitled *Burma – Through the Eyes of an American Friend*, written by John L. Christian, a former missionary in Burma, and published by the Department.

Christian completed in 1944 a full-length book entitled *Burma and the Japanese Invader*. In his preface he pays tribute to "the hearty and valuable assistance of B.R. Pearn". My close friendship with Pearn had made me aware of the work that he had put into that assistance.

A further book by Christian was published in Bombay in 1945. While it was printing two things happened. Christian was one of the few killed in the capture of Rangoon, which had come about more quickly than most of us expected. So I wrote the epilogue in Christian's book, bringing his account up to date.

Another book on Burma, published in 1945, was *The Burma We Love*, by U Kyaw Min, ICS, who had been secretary to three Premiers of Burma in turn, Dr Ba Maw, U Pu and U Saw, before the evacuation. He accompanied the Governor, Sir Reginald Dorman-Smith, to India and was a valuable member of his staff. In early 1945 I went with U Kyaw Min to Ceylon to talk to British forces which were then thought to be waiting for a seaborne invasion of Burma. At one crowded meeting a British soldier got up and said, "Why is it that you Burmese are always talking about independence and self-government? Do we ill-treat you? Aren't you satisfied with the government we give you?" My colleague was on his feet in a flash. "You British people," he said, "come to our country, you take it over, you make us learn your language, you teach us your history which is full of your own struggles for freedom, you teach us your literature which enshrines just the same principles of freedom, and then you expect us not to want freedom! If we didn't, we should be bad pupils!"

After a short, stunned silence at this impassioned outburst, there was a spontaneous burst of applause, much greater than any given to my less colourful effort.

While in Ceylon we visited Allied Headquarters in Kandy, where I was taken one afternoon by Colonel Christian into the "War Room" to hear the reports received during the last twenty-four hours, and a commentary on them by a senior staff officer. The news of the day was that British tanks had got across the Irrawaddy near Meiktila, having come down the Chindwin valley. The plan, according to the staff officer, was that if sufficient tanks got across, some would move northwards towards Mandalay and others southwards towards Rangoon. It looked even then as if the seaborne invasion might not be necessary.

Pearn returned from Simla in the early part of 1945 and it was decided that both he and I should stay with the Department, go with it when the civil government returned to Burma, and get it working as effectively as possible. It was agreed that as the European War was over I should take my family back to England for a short period of leave.

In a copy of *Burma Today* for March 1945, which has somehow survived in my papers, I see an editorial which I wrote under the heading "Britain's Best Ambassador", namely the BOR (British Other Ranks), who had been fighting for over three years to liberate Burma. I quoted reports of the quick friendships which were springing up between Burmese villagers and the BOR, and included the following paragraphs:

> . . . the people of Burma are friendly hospitable folk; they meet you on a friendly equal basis, without cringing or self-assertion. And the BOR is a friendly fellow too; he may sometimes be a rough diamond, he may swear and complain about the weather, the food, the British Government, but he shrewdly weighs up the people he meets. He likes the other fellow to have a square deal. He is fond of children, so is the Burman. He likes a joke, often a broad one, so does the Burman. He may not know a word of Burmese but he will

share a fag with the interested Burman who is watching all that is going on, and as they puff away together contentedly, something intangible will pass from the one to the other.

Soon they will be playing football together; it was British troops who brought football to Burma years earlier and the game has become a national one. Almost the brightest episode in the history of St John's College, Rangoon, concerns the great day when the boys defeated the crack army team for the Burma Championship. That was in the time when Dr Marks was principal and a young master named George Scott was on the staff, two of the best remembered Britishers who ever lived in Burma.

The British Tommy's good humour will be appreciated by the Burman of today as it was during the days of the Rangoon riots in 1939. British Tommies were helping to restore order and a small patrol of them were on duty at the crossing of Commissioner and Pagoda Roads when a bus-load of young ruffians armed with sticks and *dahs* came tearing into the city. The bus was stopped and its occupants ordered to alight – "Come on Maung, put those b—— knives in a heap." The weapons were surrendered. "Now get back into your b—— bus and hop off back to Tharrawaddy." The bus reversed its direction and the would-be rioters went off with laughter and cheers, no bad blood on either side.

The Burman is a generous, often thriftless fellow; to him money is not the chief value in life. If he likes you he will give you anything; if he doesn't, no money will get what you want from him. All reports speak of the satisfaction of the British troops at finding such an unusual attitude, for most of them have been stung in almost every other theatre of war.

The BOR is generous too, especially to those in trouble, and many reports are coming out of men sharing their rations with hungry villagers or of bringing the MO to see some sick Burmans. In one area where the troops were being maintained by air droppings, the Corps Commander gave orders that all parachutes were to be handed over to the local Burmese who were in rags. So now they walk in finest silk which many a woman in England would give much to obtain.

In another village in the hills where there was a Christian community the village pastor came to find the chaplain and explained that they were about to hold a service of thanksgiving for their liberation and would like some of the troops to attend. The service was duly held, and afterwards the Britishers present were asked to give a choral item. This was a bit of a bombshell, but after determined encouragement from the chaplain the party managed to sing several verses of "The Church's One Foundation", and were, in fact, rather pleased with themselves as several members had been able to put in the tenor and the bass. As they sat down one BOR retaliated by asking for a special item from the Baptist villagers. To the amazement of all the British party a choir stood up and sang the "Hallelujah Chorus"!

CHAPTER 9

Liberation

M y family and I had to wait for three weeks in Bombay before getting a boat for England, but during that time I was able to do some useful PR work with newspapers and radio. We were there on 3rd May 1945 when Rangoon was liberated, and that evening I gave a short broadcast over All-India Radio, telling our friends in India and Burma that we should shortly be back in the liberated city to help with the tremendous task of reconstruction.

In London I was kept busy – liaison with the Burma Office and frequent contact with Sir John Clague, the very able and wise adviser to whom the Department in Simla had reported regularly, interviews with the BBC, the MOI, the British Council, Chatham House. I attended a fortnight's training course at the BBC, which gave me some understanding of the part I would have to play in supervising the work of the Burma Broadcasting Service. I was able to arrange that U Khin Zaw, working in the Burmese section of the BBC, should return to be in charge of broadcasting, and in the meantime to ensure that he got some experience of the drama, music and talks departments. We had heard that the University library and the small library of the Burma Research Society had practically disappeared, so I visited second-hand bookshops to pick up out-of-print books on Burma, and for the modest expenditure of one hundred pounds managed to gather a very good collection of standard books on Burma and Buddhism.

Burma had been starved of books and so with the assistance of W. Lockett, who had worked with J.S. Furnivall in the pre-war bookshop, I secured the co-operation of the SPCK in a plan for a general bookshop. This was implemented early in 1946 and

opened in temporary quarters in St John's College, later trans-
ferring to a good site in the centre of the city.

With the help of the MOI, I was able to recruit a Deputy-Director
for the Department of Public Relations, a first-class newspaper
man, F.W. Benton, who was also experienced in radio news work.

Shortly after I reached England the Governor paid his first post-
liberation visit to Rangoon and on 20th June began his conference
with Burmese leaders. I was deeply interested in the outcome of
these talks and the spirit animating them, for both would affect
the task of public relations. Burmans, having been deceived by
the promises of the Japanese about independence, would be very
careful not to be deceived again. They wanted the return of civil
government as early as possible, and on this point they seemed
satisfied by the assurances of Lord Mountbatten's representative
and Sir Reginald Dorman-Smith. They were anxious that there
should be no action taken against those who had co-operated with
the Japanese. They wanted any interim government to be as
Burmese in composition as they could secure from HMG. Above
all they were eager to find an acceptable constitution for the future,
with a constitutionally elected and representative government. On
this last point they were reassured by the Governor's mention of
December 1948 as the outside date for this. So far, so good, as far
as Public Relations were concerned.

The time factor was obviously the most urgent one and my five
months in England were used to forward the plans for operating
the Department when once it got back to Burma. I knew that the
military and particularly the Civil Affairs Service (CASB) would
be urgently at work, and that Colonel Glass in charge of publicity,
who had taken part in our Simla planning, would be preparing
the way.

Bishop West arrived back in Rangoon on 9th July to find that
army chaplains and volunteer workers from the forces were hard
at work to clean up and restore the cathedral, which had been
used throughout the occupation as a factory for sauce and *saki*.
The restoration and re-furnishing were completed in time for a
great service of re-hallowing on 27th July.

An equally great occasion was a Dedication Service held on 16th October and attended by the Governor who had reached Rangoon that day. Bishop West welcomed His Excellency and a great congregation in the following words:

We are met here in this place humbly recognising God's power to direct the destinies of men and of nations. We acknowledge that human wisdom alone is not enough for the perplexities of these days. At this momentous hour His Excellency the Governor of Burma is to dedicate himself to Almighty God for the task with which he has been entrusted.

We also, with him, dedicate ourselves to serve the King of Kings. Only His standards of purity and righteousness can exalt a nation, and we pray that we may make these paramount everywhere. We are nation builders, consecrated to God and to one another, and are ourselves stones in the very building we wish to see raised by the Divine Architect of our country.

We have shown our greatness as a people in the darkest hour of adversity. Humbly we will ask God to make us great in simplicity and obedience, as we seek to bring to birth a human society in which it is normal for men to love one another.

Charity is the bond of peace. We shall love all men, not in weakness, not in sentimentality, but with the strong love that unites all to seek the good of each and the happiness of this whole country. Of the races and communities of Burma may it be said, "See how these people love one another."

Nothing can withstand a mighty onslaught of the spirit. Therefore we pray that a new spirit may be born in our midst this morning and that we may be carried on its tide to the work of national reconstruction. As this spirit rules our hearts and minds we shall be fashioning a Burma after God's own heart.

In the next few days the Governor was out among the people,

and newspaper reports spoke of "the friendliest reception everywhere". Behind the scenes, Sir Reginald was negotiating with
political leaders about the composition of the Executive Council
which was to assist him in the government of the country until
elections could be held. The main question was whether the
Burma Patriotic Front, otherwise known as the Anti-Fascist
People's Freedom League, of which General Aung San was the
leader, would co-operate. Aung San's demand for eleven seats
out of fifteen was not conceded and at the end of the month the
Governor appointed a Council of ten members, of whom only
two were British. I had hoped that Aung San would co-operate,
but I felt that he was asking too much, though I hoped that the
appointment of a smaller Council left the door open for AFPFL
membership at a later date.

The Department of Public Relations got back to Burma in the
latter part of October, and in November I flew back to join it.

There was some criticism among Burmans about the appointment of a missionary as DPR, but after a press conference or two
and visits to key people, the criticism died down, and in a public
lunch given by the Chinese to welcome their new Consul-General,
I was asked to speak. U Ba Lwin, in a later speech, said: "There
is a saying that an apple a day keeps the doctor away, and
Saya'gyi Appleton has returned to Burma with a ton of apples.
Burma is very sick and we hope that he will produce a lot more
apples like this one." At this lunch I was introduced to General
Aung San by U Tin Tut. The General was a rather brooding,
not very talkative man, but with an aura about him. He
spoke simply and forcefully. Everyone's attention was fixed on
him and he would obviously strengthen HE's Executive Council
if he could be persuaded to join. I also had a useful talk with U
Ba Pe, an old politician who was critical of the composition of the
Governor's Council.

My impression of Rangoon in those first days was that it was
only just beginning to come to life again, with everyone rather
hopeless about the difficulties involved. Heads of Departments
seemed tired and depressed, rather frustrated because the

idealistic schemes of Simla were clearly not going to get the necessary money. In a letter to my wife I said that it looked as if my job was to try to give them new faith and hope.

The Civil Affairs Service had done a good job in my estimation. Most departments had their offices, though there were constant difficulties about telephones and electricity supplies, and very little in the way of fans; communications between departments had to be carried on by messenger, for internal postal services were taking time to be reorganised. However, the external airmail was good and this greatly helped the morale of the British personnel.

One of the first things that needed to be done was to get a short survey of existing conditions, and with the help of all departments the following summary was made:

Burma Today

"When two buffaloes fight the grass in between gets the worst of it"; so runs a Burmese proverb, and that is what many Burmans think of Burma's fate in the war. Twice fought over, she has suffered as badly as any country in the world. In Rangoon it is reckoned that 60% of the commercial buildings and 30% of the residential were destroyed. Hundreds of others were looted of furniture, electric and sanitary fittings, doors, windows, roofing, sometimes even wooden staircases. Roads after three years of neglect are full of potholes; even now the general public cannot get electric light for streets or houses, though water and sewerage systems were got working very shortly after the liberation. A great deal of bomb debris still remains to be cleared, but valiant efforts have been made to remove refuse.

Outside Rangoon there is great competition for the title of Burma's most devastated town. Mandalay claims it, and the claim seems reasonable until you see Meiktila, a city of tents, or Myingyan in ruins, or Myitkyina a big sprawling village of huts, or Yenangyaung a derelict area of rusting oil derricks, or Prome flat and deserted. Almost every town has got to be rebuilt.

85

Burma's communications were knocked to pieces by the Allied air forces. Great feats of restoration are in progress. The railway lines to Prome and Mandalay are working again but it is hard work with only $1/5$ of the number of pre-war engines, and only $1/3$ of the goods wagons and hardly any of the passenger coaches. Railway travelling cannot yet be opened to the general public.

Before the war Burma had the biggest inland water fleet in the world; practically all of it went. Last year small river craft were brought in by air or overland to Kalewa and driven down the Chindwin to the Irrawaddy. Others have been brought in by sea from India, a few have been recovered from the graveyard at Bhamo, in January 19,000 tons of goods were carried, about $1/6$ of the pre-war freight.

18,000 miles of new telegraph and telephone wires have been erected on 30,000 new poles, mainly by the Army. Trained civil staff is much below the normal level and cannot carry on without military help. 200 post offices have been re-opened out of a pre-war total of 700.

In Rangoon port the import tonnage has equalled pre-war records, but the difficulty is to get enough transport to take the goods and machinery to other parts of the country.

75% of Burma's people live in villages and the lot of the villager is hard. He used to export half his rice crop, but for four years there has been no export and so no incentive to grow more than he needs. The harvest just gathered is hardly enough for Burma's own food. The countryside lives in fear of dacoits, many of them armed with automatic weapons left behind by the Japs. So far 30,000 arms have been recovered; there must be at least another 10,000 somewhere. There are no consumer goods for the villager to buy – no soap, clothing, tools – Burma needs those more than anything. Plough cattle are short owing to war losses and disease. Yet a full rice crop this next rains would do much to restore Burma's economy and help save India from hunger. A shipload of India's textiles in the next two months would encourage the villager and ensure 1,000,000 tons of rice from Burma's surplus for India next Christmas.

There is plenty of money in the country, but nothing to spend it on. So prices are inflated and will remain so until there is a steady flow of imported goods. Yet the downward trend has started; and a Burmese economic expert reckons that last month the cost of living figure has fallen from 800% above pre-war level to 600%.

Oil was once one of Burma's major industries, producing 800,000 gallons of petroleum a day, now daily production is a few hundred gallons from the old hand-dug wells. Mining for lead, silver and wolfram has not yet started again. The timber industry has re-started, but most of the wood it produces is needed for military and official purposes.

Medical services practically ceased under the Japs. New hospitals are open and working at full pressure. But we need medical supplies, especially the new medicines which the war has developed – penicillin, mepacrine, M & B, which have proved so effective in the liberation campaign.

Education also needs equipment – buildings, books, scientific apparatus, even paper, pencils and slates are woefully inadequate. Despite these difficulties there are almost as many children now attending primary schools as there were before the invasion, and many teachers are carrying on without regular salaries. But higher school education is far behind the pre-war level, with only 43 schools as against over 270 in 1941. Emergency University classes on a small scale have been organised, and some 3,000 students are expected to enroll for the University for June next, but only a small proportion of the University buildings can be released by the Army.

There is a hunger for reading material, for books of all kinds, educational and recreational. Hardly any public cinemas are functioning, most of them were destroyed in the bombing. Gramophones and records would be a boon. There are barely 500 wireless sets in the whole country. And as to fans and frigidaires, even hospitals cannot have them.

Yet there is a brighter side. There is hardly any bitterness for the devastation caused by the war; there has been hardly any outcry about the inability to redeem Japanese notes – and the Japs issued Rs562 crores worth £420 million, over 30 years of Burma's national revenue. The Burmese are an amazingly philosophic people. They are great improvisers too – you should see the things they are making out of old war scrap – ploughs, nails, tools and utensils of all kinds. You should see the ramshackle buses with boiling radiators that are tackling private road traffic. Up-country the spirit of self-effort is better than in Rangoon, and there is more talk there of reconstruction than politics. In Mandalay Burmans are making bricks because they cannot get enough timber to rebuild their houses, tho' Burma is a land of timber. Burmans are wanting to go into business more – a little group of Burmese businessmen have formed an industrial corpora-tion; young Burmans are doing well in the petrol and kerosene retail trade. Young men everywhere are thinking hard about Burma's future – political and economic. Here and there Burmans are replacing Indians in hard and dirty labour.

Much still remains to be done before Burma becomes once more her happy and prosperous self, but much has already been done. The Army has done a grand job of work in the initial stages of rehabilitation, and without its aid progress would have been far slower.

But Burma cannot depend on the Army indefinitely. It must and indeed is already beginning to work out its own salvation. The times are hard and there is a terrific struggle still ahead.

But there is always real satisfaction in a fight against great odds.

Shortly after my return, the Governor was to make a tour of Central Burma and it seemed a great opportunity for me to gauge conditions outside Rangoon, so I was invited to accompany him. We visited Meiktila by plane and continued by air to Mandalay, landing on a very rough airstrip. Mandalay had been very badly damaged in the 1942 fighting and had hardly recovered. We went on to Shwebo and Katha, and returned to Sagaing, where we boarded an old Irrawaddy steamer which had been sunk twice during the war and recovered on each occasion. Leaving Sagaing for our return journey by boat to Prome we got on to a sandbank and had to wait there until two tugs pulled us off. While the steamer was on the sandbank HE and I and one or two others went ashore and spent an hour in a village on the bank. In another letter to my wife I have the following comment:

> HE was at his best and became a farmer once more. The Headman too was bright and intelligent, and they had a cheery conversation with me as interpreter. It was a great thing to get HE into a village to see conditions and what needs to be done, and I was able to press home some of my own ideas about village life and health. After dinner, back on the boat, he sat and talked about the soil as the common link between people of all nations, and spoke almost lovingly of husbandry and caring for the soil almost as if it were a human being. He wants to see agricultural societies developed throughout Burma, with something like the flower and vegetable shows in an English village. He certainly has a vision for the Burmese farmer, and I have never liked him so much as I did last night as we sat talking together under the stars. This trip up country has been most valuable, and has convinced me that reconstruction must be our theme more than politics.

Men in the forces were very good at getting into friendly relationship with the Burmese people. An East and West Association had been formed and I took an early opportunity of asking if I might address it. A day or two later I received the following letter:

OF PARAMOUNT IMPORTANCE   January 1946
MR G. APPLETON
DIRECTOR, PUBLIC RELATIONS DEPARTMENT
GOVT: OF BURMA

Mr Appleton!

I heard your most disgusting talk at the EAST and west Association (PROPAGANDA ASSOCIATION would be better). You think that WE BURMANS are all 'suckers' EH!! You are damm well mistaken, Mr Crafty Blooming Appleton. Ho! Ho! Most of us BURMANS who heard your slimy, slippery and soft propaganda talk – knew at once that your 'move' was a 'STOOP TO CONQUER' stunt. We know you were 'soft soaping us' Appleton – Yes! We could see right through your crafty but loose Propaganda.

You fancy you're smart and you know plenty about our fine country – THATS JUST IT! You know bugger all – Perhaps Appleton you'd like to know whats in store for you British IMPERIALISTS – Hah! Don't wait for it Appleton if you want to save your insipid self from being punctured or badly handled all you can Do for the Better of our ESTEEMED BURMA is GET OUT! MALDOM! You are seeing what is happening in our poor ORIENTAL brother land INDONESIA – DON'T BE SURPRISED IF THE SAME thing happens in BURMA – SOME DAY – IT IS NOT SO FAR OFF – WE BURMANS AND INDIANS UNITEDLY WILL KICK OUT you blood sucking BRITISHERS AND your GODDAM children the Eurasians – Ho! Ho! Ho!

The eyes of BURMA and its growing generation is opening with speed and certainty – the PINNACLE OF BRITISH and European superiority is crumbling to dust – BEWARE the pent up strength of all Asiatics is well near bursting point – THE STRUGGLE FOR TOTAL FREEDOM OF ALL SUBJECT PEOPLES IS SURE TO BEGIN IN THE NOT DISTANT FUTURE. When we triumph Appleton – don't forget we shall mark you down as one of the War Criminals: ———

> DOWN WITH FACISTS, IMPERIALISTS AND THEIR
>   LOUSY TOOLS.
> LONG LIVE AUNG SAN, THAN TUN AND THE
>   REST OF OUR CHERISHED FREEDOM LOVERS
> DOWN WITH TWERPS AND LOW DOWN PUNKS
> LIKE APPLETON —
>
> DOH BUMAH!!!

It was fairly clear to anyone who knew English and Burmese that this had not been written by a Burman. My own opinion was that it was written by a Communist infiltrator. It encouraged me to feel that something I had said had evidently gone home.

The PR Department had made a good start in the CASB period with Colonel Glass in charge. He had got a Burmese staff together with quite a good Anglo-Burman as editor of a daily paper in English called *The Liberator* with a daily circulation of about five thousand. A weekly Burmese paper called *Khit Thit* was also published and distributed as widely as possible throughout the country. Information Centres had been established in some twenty places. A radio station was in operation, and a number of mobile film units, which were only able to show news or educational films brought in from outside. All this initial provision had been handed over to the Department. We worked under considerable difficulties as the five main sections of the Department were in different buildings, and integration and direction were not easy. However, a weekly meeting of the Sectional Heads was held when our planning was thought out.

Colonel Glass had arranged that Reuters press telegrams should be handled by the Department and distributed to the Burmese newspapers, so international news was regularly published, and the liaison with the Burmese editors established. Shortage of newsprint was another link, and I was constantly in touch with Singapore, London and Calcutta about supplies, which when they came were divided as fairly as possible between ourselves and the independent newspapers.

There was a further link with editors, not such a happy one, for false reports and rumours were constantly appearing, and what seemed to be a campaign of vilification of the police. Hardly a day passed without my Information Officer, U Khin Maung, interviewing some editor, after making careful enquiries about the accuracy of the reports.

Before returning from England I had been able to recruit a very competent English journalist, F.W. Benton, who soon improved the quality of our English daily. I think it was before he arrived that we changed the name to *New Times of Burma*. Pearn and I wrote most of the leaders, though occasionally we had help from the various departments of government. As neither he nor I were long-term government servants, we were rather more critical of policies and decisions, and did our best to see that reasonable criticism was reasonably answered. If there were some point under heated discussion, either he or I would write a letter to our own newspaper, using a Burmese pseudonym, and the other would answer it in the name of government. This stimulated letters from ordinary readers of the paper.

I have mentioned that, while the Governor was still in Simla, a very able Burman, U Khin Zaw, had been sent to train with the BBC. Before returning from England I had arranged the date when he would join the Department. His coming meant that the radio station could deal with more than news bulletins and official talks. Drama and poetry were included, in both English and Burmese. I had always hoped that the Buddhist Sangha, meaning the Community of Buddhist monks, might take a hand in the raising of morale, the deepening of the Buddhist emphasis on the Noble Eightfold Path, and in getting all sections of the nation to work together for peace and reconstruction. We were not very successful in doing this, although an officer of the Department, U Sein Ywet, was charged with the task of getting in touch with abbots and monks. In several talks given by myself in both English and Burmese, I tried to emphasise the part which Buddhism could play in the national life. In a short series of talks entitled *Let the Figures Speak*, I meditated on the Three Gems, the Four Truths, the Five Great Precepts, the Eightfold Path, and then went on to deal with some of the statistics of Burmese life – birth figures, infant mortality, crime figures, etc.

In early April 1946 U Sein Ywet and I did a seven-days tour in the Delta in which we visited two towns and ten villages, listening to government officers, elders, headmen, and representatives from nearly a hundred villages, which convinced me that much more needed to be done for the towns and villages outside Rangoon. My report on this tour concluded with the words: "I shall be grateful for any suggestions as to how this Department may co-operate in helping to meet the desperately urgent situation that is about to develop in the Delta villages."

One of the most urgent things throughout Burma was to encourage rice production. Before the war Burma had produced seven million tons of rice a year, about half of which was exported. The cultivators became discouraged during the Japanese occupation and lack of export facilities, with the result that much land went out of cultivation. Through the *New Times of Burma* and the *Burmese Weekly* we did everything possible to appeal for a concerted effort to restore the cultivation of rice to the pre-war level. I prepared the following appeal for the Governor to make to the whole nation:

There is going to be a serious shortage of food all over the world during the next year. Burma is fortunate in that she has enough for her own needs, though she was only just able to ensure this during the last harvest. Other countries are now asking Burma for help: our great neighbour India particularly is going to be in sore need. I appeal to farmers and cultivators to plant every possible acre during the coming planting season. I assure them that every extra basket of rice produced will be immediately sent to the countries in need. They have the money to buy it, if we will produce it. I appeal to the people of Burma to ecconomise as far as possible in the consumption of rice and foodstuffs; so that we may have some surplus to send to a hungry world. I suggest that in our social hospitality we should follow an example set by India during the war years and limit the number of guests at all such functions to fifty. In every way possible let us discipline ourselves so as to help feed a hungry world. In this way Burma can win an honoured place in the United Nations and live up to her recognised standards of charity and hospitality.

This appeal was plugged in our two newspapers and on radio, and in special leaflets for the thousands of villages. The appeal with this accompanying publicity played a useful part in the achievement of one million tons surplus as a result of the planting season of 1946, earning not only welcome export currency but also considerable goodwill.

At about the same time, April 1946, U Tin Tut, the brilliant and most able indigenous member of the Burmese Civil Service, who won his place by competition in the earlier days of the ICS, decided to leave Government service and go into politics. He had been closely associated with U Saw before the war and had accompanied the Governor to India. His decision encouraged many of us, for he was a man of great integrity as well as ability. Both before and after this decision I was able to benefit from his friendship and advice. His assassination early in 1947 was a tremendous tragedy, which I and many others still mourn. One of my great regrets is that in the period immediately after liberation Burmese leaders and people generally seemed more interested in the political future of Burma than in the urgent task of reconstruction. This however had to be accepted as a fact and due attention paid to it.

All these nationalist aspirations found a focus in Aung San, who had distinguished himself in his university days as the leader of a well-organised strike of university students. He then became a leader of the *thakin* group – *thakin* was the name given to a European, equivalent to *sahib* in India – and in 1940 fled from the country and was later joined by about thirty others. These young *thakins* accompanied the Japanese when they invaded Burma in early 1942. It is important to note that these young men were not so much-pro-Japanese or anti-British as intensely Burman. Later, when they realised Japan's true intentions, Aung San and the small Burmese army, backed by an underground movement, decided to come over to the British, a very courageous step when you realise their numbers, and their limited arms. Their exploits have been greatly exaggerated by Burmese writers, but I don't think British writers have adequately recognised the courage demanded to revolt, or possibly we have been jealous for the unswerving loyalty through defeat as well as victory of Karens, Kachins and Chins.

Aung San awakened a martial spirit amongst the Burmans, and the young men looked up to him with intense loyalty. In their new patriotism and hero-worship they were ready to undergo discipline and do hard work, two duties which in the past they had been accused of lacking. Aung San was a real leader with high ideals. I heard him say at one gathering that there were certain things he thought ought to be done, and he was going to do them, whether people followed him or not. At a great mass meeting at the Shwe Dagon Pagoda in January 1946, some twenty thousand people attended to hear him speak, I being one of them. It looked as if the stage was set for a carefully planned and timed entry of the leader, on the totalitarian model, but when the time came Aung San passed almost unobserved through the people to the platform, and quietly began his speech. There was no ostentation, no rehearsed ovation. His speech lasted three and a half hours; most of it he read quickly in an even tone. There were surveys of history, patriotic passages, vitriolic outbursts, Socialist and Marxist doctrine, for the manuscript was a composite one. Occasionally Aung San put his manuscript aside, and then he spoke with fire and humour.

It soon became clear that there was a struggle going on within his party, between the Communists, who wanted violent measures, completely unscrupulous, and the more moderate Socialists, aided by one or two older leaders who saw the promise of Aung San. In a review of the political situation written in the spring of 1946, I concluded with the statement, "If Aung San can be detached from the Communists it will be a great day for Burma."

One afternoon the Governor summoned me to Government House and informed me that he had instructions to institute proceedings against Aung San for an alleged murder in the early days of the Japanese invasion of Burma, and instructed me to prepare the case to justify this to the country. I was deeply disturbed by this and quite convinced that it would lead to serious trouble. After a troubled night I went to Government House next morning and said to HE that I was convinced that this would be a disastrous step and that if it was decided to take it I must resign on the spot and announce in public my reasons for doing so. A day or two later he had come round to my view and, after consultation with London, had decided to drop the matter.

The Communists, under two very astute leaders, had advanced their cause very considerably by working within the Anti-Fascist People's Freedom League and trading on Aung San's popularity. It was not till after Aung San and AFPFL had victoriously entered the Governor's Executive Council in October 1946, after an organised strike of police and government officials, that the split with the Communists came. When it did, Aung San and his friends were outspoken and firm, and Communist popularity waned, even in the country districts where they had organised cultivators' unions, advocated the non-payment of taxes and rent, and promised the confiscation of land and its division among the landless and debt-ridden peasants. I doubt if Communism will ever have any chance in Burma, unless by intimidation and violence, for the Burmans have no class distinctions to be inflamed, and they resent, as a slur against their national religion, the stereotyped Communist doctrine that religion is the opiate of the people.

Aung San's courage and leadership were shown again in January 1947, when his political opponents, including the Communists, stirred up agitation against the London Agreement before Aung San had time to get back to Burma and explain the facts. He stood by his convictions and had little difficulty in keeping public confidence. Being in office had not been easy, for he inherited situations which he and his supporters created when in opposition. They had used the police in the political struggle and then found that the police were no longer reliable. They had backed up huge demands for cost of living allowances and then found that they had to find the money. They had insisted that their youth organisations should be organised on a semi-military basis, and other parties had followed suit. Through hard experience they were learning the price of government and the cost of leadership.

Sir Reginald Dorman-Smith sympathised with the general outlook and tried to prepare people for the necessary discussion and negotiations which would have to precede any expression of national opinion and the consequent negotiation with the British Government. The Governor constantly emphasised five necessary steps to self-government: (1) decide who shall vote; (2) compile electoral rolls; (3) hold a free election; (4) agree on the constitution; and (5) settle future relationship with Great Britain.

The departure of Sir Reginald Dorman-Smith was regretted by those who shared his emphasis on the political issues. In many ways he understood the Burman, and his relationship with the pre-war leader of the Executive Council, U Saw, was a close one. Sir Reginald told me that on the night before U Saw went to London in the hopes of getting a promise of some kind of independence for Burma from Winston Churchill in return for full co-operation in the war, he had warned U Saw that the hopes of success were very slender. Sir Reginald added, "If you don't get what you are going for you will be a great nuisance when you return." To which U Saw replied, "You are right, and you will probably have to put me in prison. But if ever you are in real difficulties, send the car down to the jail about midnight and I will come and show you how to get out of them."

Sir Reginald also told me that on one occasion when there was suspicion of corruption about a certain appointment, he had called

U Saw to him and said, "I hear that you have accepted Rs5,000
for this appointment. Is it true?" To which U Saw replied, "Oh,
Your Excellency, how could they say such a thing." HE then asked,
"Saw, how much did you get?" The reply was, "Not Rs5,000,
Your Excellency, but Rs25,000, but now that you speak to me
about it I will not take it." The sums involved seem very small
in comparison with corruption dimensions in other East Asian
countries. This, in my opinion, was fairly general in Burma and
the smaller level of bribery was due to the influence of Buddhism.

With the departure of Sir Reginald Dorman-Smith, Sir Henry
Knight was appointed as Interim Governor until a permanent
appointment should be made. He was experienced in government
administration. Right from the start he visited every department
of government activity, listening to the plans of the officers
concerned, and issued instructions for emphasis on reconstruction
and efficiency. He had a sure knack of putting his finger on the
heart of matters under discussion, and of asking questions which
helped to clarify planning and decisions. I could not help feeling
that if we could have had him from the moment of the return of
Civil Government Burma would have been in a happier and more
disciplined condition, ready to see the real task which the nation
would have to face as soon as its political future was decided.

The announcement of the appointment of Sir Hubert Rance was
received with interest, for many had grown to feel his friendliness
and simple directness during the period of military government.
A very interesting incident took place shortly after the announcement. One day I received a note from the Indian High Commissioner saying that a press cable had been delivered to him
which was obviously meant for me, and he therefore sent it on.
It consisted of about one thousand words and purported to be an
interview with the new Governor, putting down to him statements which would obviously arouse considerable concern with
Government authorities in London. The telegram was unsigned.
I took it to Sir Henry Knight and we tried to trace its origin back
through the telegraph service. It turned out to be a report from
the representative of the *New Light of Burma*. Simultaneously we

had been in touch with Sir Hubert and had discovered that he did indeed give an interview to the representative in London and had spoken "off the cuff" to quite an extent but not justifying the outright statement attributed to him. A further discussion with Sir Henry led us to agree that the telegram must be delivered, but that I should take it in person to the Editor and see if something less embarrassing could be agreed.

The Editor read the cable through and asked what steps I proposed to take. I told him I should have to publish Sir Hubert's disclaimer, and warned him that an unedited publication would endanger implementation of an appointment from which Burmans expected so much, and would also lead to an unhappy relationship between the paper and the government. The Editor was in a very reasonable mood and asked what I could suggest. I suggested that he should let me write a version of the press telegram in a more discreet way, trying to keep the reporter's expectations and hopes. The Editor agreed and so a day or two later my edited statement was published in Burmese on the front page of the *New Light of Burma* in a translation which U Khin Maung, my talented and faithful Information Officer, approved. On the day Sir Hubert arrived in Rangoon he sent for me to thank me for the way in which this delicate matter had been handled.

I was eager that Burma should remain within the British Commonwealth, for the sake of Burma and not in the interests of Britain and her trade. I tried to explain to people the real meaning of Dominion status with its opportunity of self-government within a wider membership which would always come to its support. What seemed to me a golden opportunity came to hand largely through Pearn's connections with the History department in the University, to which he had now returned. A history lecturer, U Myo Min, brought to him a book that he had written about the subject. It was a splendidly factual and clear analysis of Dominion status, and he wished to find a publisher. It was clear to me that we dared not and could not use money from the Department. I therefore cabled the Burma Section of the India Office asking for a loan of £1000 to publish the book as it stood in Burmese, also a much shorter book, and finally a leaflet giving the gist of its arguments. The reply from London was in the negative – to me a tragic decision.

Aung San and his supporters were demanding full independence, but I happened to know that they would have been content, possibly even pleased, to be granted Dominion status. Their thinking was that they must ask for more than what they really hoped to get. I felt unhappy and critical once more at the decision of Mr Attlee and his government to grant independence without further effort.

An incident on the frontier near Myitkyina confirmed my judgement. One of the semi-independent Chinese generals had come over the border from China and encamped not far from Myitkyina. Every diplomatic effort was made to get him and his army to retire back over the frontier, but without success. In the end the threat was made of calling a squadron of the RAF from Singapore to ensure withdrawal. The threat proved successful. I wanted to publicise this outcome without making the implied criticism too hostile. People in Burma would then see the protection afforded by continuing membership in the Commonwealth. I was not allowed to make any public mention of the matter.

Over the whole of my year in Burma after liberation, nationalist feeling had been worked up, fomented cleverly by the Communists under Than Tun. The earlier attempt to discredit the police had not succeeded, although the way the police treated the public was by no means satisfactory. The parties in opposition to Government now decided to infiltrate the police and also to influence government servants. The result was a general strike early in September 1946 in which police and government workers camped out in the Shwe Dagon Pagoda where they were guarded against any persuasive attempts from authority. I managed to get in hundreds of leaflets, through a few loyal workers in the Department, but these were either destroyed or had little effect; or more likely, were not adequately distributed out of fear.

Benton and his Assistant Editor managed to keep the *New Times of Burma* going and we could still use the radio, but it was obvious that things were moving to a climax, and I was desperately afraid that violence would develop throughout the country.

On the morning of 17th September I went to see U Tin Tut to get his estimation of the situation. The Executive Council under Sir Paw Tun were inert and helpless, and later that morning I went to the Governor to say that I did not think we could hold the situation any longer without grave risk, and advised him to call for the resignation of the Executive Council. He did this on the same day, with the result that the situation became much calmer and negotiations opened for a new Executive Council which would include General Aung San as its leader.

During the next ten days negotiations and discussions went on, in some of which I was the messenger for Sir Hubert, particularly in the efforts to get U Saw and U Ba Maw into the Council, successful in the first case but not in the second. The new Council was appointed on 26th September, and from that date on General Aung San was the right-hand man of the Governor and the hope of the whole nation. Soon after his appointment he went to the north to meet representatives of the non-Burman races, and in effect asked them to state their own terms for participation in a Union of Burma.

The settlement brought great relief to the whole of the Public Relations Department and clearly the indigenous officers of it needed to be trained for the new situation. Training courses were arranged and at one of them General Aung San himself presided and listened to my opening speech to the PROS. Later he called me to a meeting of the Executive Council and asked me to say what I thought the principles of the Department should be and how they could be implemented. I commenced to talk in English, whereupon he said, "Speak in Burmese." I did so and after a few minutes he said, "Good enough, now you can continue in English." It was however becoming quite clear that the Department would now be used much more explicitly for publicity and propaganda, and this, combined with failing health because of amoebic dysentery and exhaustion, led to my resignation.

Readers of these pages may feel curious as to how I combined my religious convictions and duties with those of the Director of Public Relations. On my return to Burma in November 1945 I was Archdeacon of Rangoon, but it soon became clear that my main attention would have to be devoted to working for understanding and peace. So in February 1946 I resigned as Archdeacon. Every Sunday I took certain Christian services, and I was always available for individual Christian clergy who wanted friendship and advice. Every Sunday I also contributed a religious meditation to the *New Times of Burma* under the heading "Thought for Today", following on a Buddhist meditation for the preceding day.

I left Burma sadly, though glad at the prospect of being reunited with my family in England. One of the last things I was able to do was to help in the preparations for a Service of Reconciliation to be held at the Burma end of the Burma-Siam railway line, both in the preparation of the details of the service and the plans for its publicity. Unfortunately I was not able to be present at the actual service in January 1947.

A Burmese proverb sums up what I felt about Burma: "If you fall in love when young you can never forget through ten thousand years." It expresses my love of Burma and its people which continued well into old age.

In this context I would like to pay a tribute to the British officers who served Burma during the years it was part of the Common-wealth. These officers of the Indian Civil Service and later the Burma Civil Service, were immensely devoted people. There was not any suggestion of racial pride in their relationships with Burmese colleagues. Part of the responsibility for this lies with the innate friendliness and courtesy of the peoples of Burma, and behind that the long record of the Buddhist tradition. I doubt if Burma will get any more devoted duty and service from any other group of officers. Many of them worked late into the night with their files and their problems of decisions, or if they were in the Judicature, their judgements. Their service, as well as that of government officers in the much bigger country of India, is rightly commemorated in a memorial tablet in the cloisters of Westminster Abbey. I would like to make one special mention in this general tribute – to Philip Nash who was the Secretary to Sir Hubert Rance. During the critical weeks of growing unrest and public strike, he and I were in daily touch, trying to understand the situation and see what could be done to solve the difficulties.

After my return to England I was able to continue my interest in Burma's future, for when General Aung San and his colleagues came to London for consultations with the British Government, Mr Attlee asked me to 10 Downing Street to introduce the various members to him. Several months later, when General Aung San and six of his colleagues were assassinated on 19th June, 1947, the Burma Office of the British Government got in touch with me several days before the public announcement was made. It was a hard blow to all who loved Burma, for at one stroke the country lost outstanding leaders, men of real character and great promise, whom she could ill afford to lose. U Aung San was succeeded by an intimate and trusted colleague, Thakin Nu, who had been Secretary of the AFPFL. He was a gentle character, who perhaps would have been happier as the abbot of a Buddhist monastery. He might still be a force for peace and unity in a country that calls itself *The Union of Burma*. When I got the news of the assassination I had a heavy foreboding that U Saw was involved, and this indeed proved to be the case. He was tried and executed, protesting that he had nothing to do with the affair. Afterwards Thakin Nu told the Bishop of Rangoon that had U Saw confessed, he would not have been executed.

CHAPTER 10

Family Adventures

A
t various points in this book of memories and some attempt at self-examination in a long and adventurous life, I have mentioned the love and help I received from my wife Marjorie. After she died in Eastertide 1980 at the age of seventy-eight, I found in her desk a handwritten letter to our three children, which she put together in Jerusalem at the repeated request of Rachel, our elder daughter.

Before allowing her own words to express her story, it might be helpful to speak of the policy and practice of nearly all missionary societies fifty years ago. I have already mentioned the stipulation that before I could qualify for married status I should have passed two language exams. We both accepted this without question, and a marriage allowance was duly added to my salary. There was also a scale for children's allowances. It was accepted as a general practice that children would be better educated in the sending country after the age of seven. As each period of service in Burma was five years, it meant that children left at home hardly knew their parents. So Rachel at six years and Margaret at five years were left in England after our second furlough, and generous help was provided for them by the organiser of a preparatory school. After this last furlough we paid a last sad visit to the school and found a small girl crying her heart out. When I enquired what was the matter she said, "I can't remember what my mummy looks like."

In July 1939 it seemed clear to me that war was inevitable. I asked for special leave and borrowed the eighty pounds for a short-term return ticket on the letter-mail route to the UK. Marjorie was already in England convalescing after a serious operation. Tim (aged two) was with her.

So without more ado, I gratefully include what she entitled "Salute to Rachel, Margaret and Tim".

In 1939 we were all in England when Pop came back from Burma to decide what we should do – stay in England during the war, or go back to Burma.

Bishop George West thought that we should stay, but Pop knew that he, at least, must return, and finally he and I decided that we should *all* return, mainly because a separation when you three were still so young – and needing parents and not grandparents to care for you – seemed not the right course.

We had to wait for some months in order to get a passage and finally set off on my birthday in January. We embarked at Liverpool and the Mersey was full of ice and so cold. We had to wait for some days until a convoy of ships was ready. We could only travel at the rate of the slowest ship, and once out in the Irish Sea were "blacked out". I think that there were about thirty ships in the convoy.

I remember two lady missionaries, who were also returning to Burma, saying, "Well, of course we shall arrive safely because we are going out to do the Lord's work." When Pop said, "What about all those other people in the convoy, doesn't the dear Lord care about them too?" this worried the two ladies considerably, and I rather think after that they either thought that we were faithless, or became a little apprehensive themselves!

You children were excited on the journey to Gibraltar and kept running from side to side of the boat looking out for the small destroyers that were guarding the convoy. We could not undress for a week in case of a submarine attack, and you all got a little cross, I remember. Pop had bought a large inflated life jacket for me to wear in case of our ship being sunk, in which case you were all to hold on to the cords round my waist, and he would swim round and act as a watchdog!

We were very glad to pass Gibraltar into the relatively calm waters of the Mediterranean, and that night we were able to undress and sleep in peace. I remember a terrific noise in the night, and thinking that a submarine must have got through after all, dashed into Pop's cabin to be told that it was only coal being poured into the bunkers below decks! We still had to keep our life jackets at the foot of our bunks in case of raids.

Once through the Suez Canal and into the Red Sea the "black out" rule was relaxed somewhat and you children then enjoyed the warmth and the swimming pool, and the kindly Scots captain who greeted Mig every morning with "Hoo's Maggie the morn?" and the nice stewardess who had taught Mig to reply in a Scots voice, "Maggie's fine, thank you for spierin' (asking)."

Do you remember looking over the ship's side at the flying fish, and the phosphorus gleaming along the side of the ship at night – and of course looking for the Southern Cross in the stars at night? Pop and I remember going up to the captain's cabin after you had gone to bed and eating lovely *bala chaung* sandwiches. I think that nice Captain Meek went down with his ship later on in the war.

I remember Tim and another small American boy racing round the decks, Tim saying, "Let's go wound and wound the deck," and the other saying, "No, let's go yound and yound."!

We were glad to reach Rangoon which at that time of the year, early March, was very hot, and so Pop sent us up to Taungyi in the Shan States where we stayed with a delightful elderly American missionary, Miss Hughes. You two girls went to an American school for a while and were puzzled by the American accent. When Rachel was asked to spell "ba-na-na" Margaret took over and said, "It's all right Rachel, she means 'baa-naa-naa'!" Then the nice teacher taught you a little rhyme in American and English – "The little calf (căf) went down the path (păth) in a minute and a half (haf) to take a bath (băth)."

When we returned to Rangoon, you and Margaret went to the Diocesan School where Miss Hardy was headmistress. I expect you remember being taken and fetched each day – some four or five miles – sometimes by me and sometimes by Ruth Donnison

106

– and how you used to fume when we picked up the Khin Zaw's children who were always late.

I expect you remember the lovely lake at the end of our road, and the rides in the sampan, or going out with the Moothams when Maria used to say, at the end of an excursion, "Rachel never stops talking!"

Then, do you remember Chief Justice Mosley who lived just below us? He used regularly to stop me and congratulate me on your charming manners and pretty frocks! It was his old Persian runner that we used to tie up our bundles when we came out of Burma – I expect you remember that we still had it in Leatherhead.

I expect you remember the students at "Holy Cross", Maung Pe, now Bishop of Akyab, John Aung Hla, Bishop of Mandalay, and Ba Maw, Bishop of Toungoo – all Pop's students, who have done so well and were so faithful during the Japanese occupation of Burma.

Do you remember Stephen the gardener, and darling Bessie your nanny who still writes to me, and whom we found again when we went into Burma on our way home from Australia? Everybody whom we met at that time remembered you all with great affection.

We had two lovely years in Rangoon before the Japanese invasion. You all learned to swim and dive at the Kokine Swimming Club, and you and Mig became Girl Guides at the school.

Do you remember Uncle Charles Lane building a bomb-proof wall outside the kitchen? – and how you were so excited when the raids came because it meant Pop and I were able to stop work and play idiotic games with the three of you?!

Pop used to go off some evenings to drive an ambulance, and then Christmas 1942 – when Rangoon was badly bombed. We had gone to Uncle Charles for Christmas lunch and were sad to find that Aunt Edie Mann did not appear. She was matron of the large Dufferin Hospital which was bombed on Christmas Day, and in fear eighty of her Burmese nurses fled, leaving her with two English sisters, and a few good Anglo-Indian nurses. That evening Pop and his students went to the hospital to help her, going in white cassocks, which was silly, because in the morning they returned covered in blood and dirt! I went next morning with Bessie and the sweeper and helped Edith. Her laundry had been bombed, and the hospital was full of casualties, as well as the maternity block. I found an Englishman wandering round asking if he could help; I said, "If you can stand the sight of blood, and filthy bandages, without being sick come on, but if you are sick you'll have to clean it up yourself!" I remember trying to help one of the sisters dress a badly wounded back – something I had never thought I could do. I don't think I finished it! One of the doctors managed to get the laundry going again and in a few days the hospital was evacuated to a small country town.

At the end of January Pop decided to go south to our villages, and sent us up the Irrawaddy to Maymyo. Do you remember saying goodbye to him on the wharf with Tim's tiny topi sitting on top of his head to amuse you? Captain Tizzard and his wife and baby took us on board. The steamer was full of refugees and many Chinese – the railway was full of troops moving south so that it was easier to go by river. You all thought it was great fun – going off for a hot weather holiday!

On the third day out, Rachel went down with a high temperature and swellings in the groin. An Indian doctor on board said it was appendicitis and wanted to operate, but Captain Tizzard and I were doubtful, and in any case the boat was ill equipped and dirty. We were due at Chauk, an old field town, next day and Captain Tizzard advised me to take Rachel to the hospital there, but warned me that he could not delay his sailing for more than a few hours. I managed to find an old taxi, and Rachel and I rushed to this gleaming American hospital only to find it apparently empty! At last I found a young doctor who gave me a curious look, but I begged him to examine Rachel, which he did, and then looked up and said, "My dear lady, your daughter has bubonic plague!" I said, "But what shall I do, can you take her in?" at which he smiled sadly and said, "I'm afraid not, I have orders to blow up this hospital, at eight o'clock tomorrow morning!" But he was very kind, and brought me all the M & B tablets he could find, with instructions to get you back to bed, and to keep you from other children, and give you M & B every four hours until you were sick, and then try them again very slowly. So we dashed back to the steamer which was just pulling out from the bank – you two were jolly glad to see us.

That night we were stuck on a sandbank in the middle of the river, and a small Chindwin paddle steamer came along to take us off until the tide rose again. I carried Rachel, and Margaret held on to me, and I hoped Tim would be hanging on to Mig, but when we reached the small steamer Tim was missing. So many refugees had panicked and he was lost in the throng. Having settled Rachel in a corner and piled our luggage round her and left you, Mig, on guard, I struggled back against the refugees and climbed the gangway again to find Tim looking a little bewildered in the midst of a seething mass of humanity but remarkably calm, and soon we were back on the small boat. When the tide turned, we all had to struggle back to the large Irrawaddy steamer again. In two days' time we reached Pakoku where many of the Anglo-Burmans begged me to disembark and try to walk out of Burma with them, but Rachel was still very sick and I said I would go on to Mandalay and hope to find a doctor there.

We reached Mandalay and I went straight to the Winchester Mission where dear Willie Garrad looked shocked to see me and said in a scandalised voice, "Oh, but you can't possibly stay here" – it was a Brotherhood you see! However, he soon found a car which took us up the hill to Maymyo, and Madriya and his wife and daughter came with us. We found an old "godown" and all slept that night side by side on the floor. Tim was happy for he was very fond of Madriya. Next day we found a good army doctor who examined Rachel and said with care she would soon be well, the M & B had done its work, and then to add to our trouble you all went down with scarlet fever – caught on the boat I expect.

By this time people were organising treks out of Burma and the chaplain's wife begged me to take you three out by a plane leaving Shwebo next day, but you were all too sick, and so we stayed on and I hastily sewed boiler suits against mosquitoes if and when we could trek out. However, it wasn't necessary, for within a week with a sudden shout of joy (while I was in a tin bath!) I heard you three yelling "Daddy". We then elected to stay on and opened up those two houses (Bombay Burma) for thirty officers who had been turned out of hospital from the fighting lower down, and Pop opened up St Michael's school for about eighty soldiers until they were fit enough to go back to duty. One of our fine teachers elected to stay and run that, while we did what we could, with Madriya's help, to feed our officers. Do you remember helping us? Pop would go out in the morning scouring the countryside for meat and vegetables, and sometimes having to dive into a culvert if there was a raid; meanwhile the officers would shepherd us into trenches and play games until the raid was over. I remember an officer diving into a culvert during a raid – he thought he had been hit again but it was only a lump of mud on his seat! There were no anti-aircraft missiles but the soldiers erected large bamboos to deceive the Japs.

Finally the army ordered you children and myself out – the Japs were getting very close. We were told to take food and water on a train going down to Mandalay and I remember taking the Mothers' Union tea urn! When we reached Mandalay it was in flames, Auntie Edie Mann's hospital from Rangoon had been evacuated to Mandalay, and again it was bombed, so she, clad in a man's shirt and shorts and tennis shoes, was flown out to Calcutta.

We stayed on the train for nearly a week, first being drawn down the track to Myinge where dear Jack Cardew took us into his house while the railway was repaired. Do you remember the swimming pool and a snake in it?! Later we were taken slowly up to Myitkyina. Tim was fascinated at seeing overturned engines on the side of the line, and you girls were a little anxious as you saw me and a nice Salvation Army wife tear down the track when the train stopped to get water from the engine! We used to stand it in the window to cool down so that we could get a cool drink – it was April and temperatures were up in the nineties and there

110

was no water on the train. At one station a nice old Burmese woman brought us limes – her old arms scratched by the thorns – she asked no payment, it was her gift of love to this train load of refugees.

We wondered how Pop was getting on in Maymyo without us, but dear Madriya and his wife had stayed to look after him and the soldiers. Pop, as the Japs drew nearer, had organised the men with one of our Mission doctors, and they hoped to walk out up the Chindwin Valley and over into Assam, but unfortunately for Pop his feet had gone septic, and at the end he was dumped on Myitkyina airfield for a night and a day, waiting for a plane to take him over to Dibrugarh in Assam. Fortunately a lone plane touched down, and took him off. Then of course he was in hospital in Assam for some weeks.

Meanwhile we four arrived in Myitkyina. Do you remember waiting on the station in the rain? The rains had just started. I dashed across to the DC's house to tell him that this train with several hundred refugees was standing in the station, and some shelter must be found for them. He looked up from his desk and said, "My good woman, where do you think I can put them?" I said, "What about opening an old cinema, or even a church? There are old women and children sitting in the pouring rain." At last he sent for a *chaprassi* and sent him with me to look for something, but on the way I found nice Mr Dickensen, an American from the University in Rangoon. You used to play with his children, do you remember? I told him of the plight of all the refugees on the station, then he thought for a minute and said, "Well, I'm running a camp at the moment, and have over a thousand in it, but I'm sure we can squash you all in somehow." So back we went to the station and with joy picked you all up and out we went to his refugee camp.

The camp was near the river which gave you all great joy – it had to be our bathroom – but that was fun to you too. We lay side by side on the floor all over the house – there must have been a dozen or more of us, including nice old Ma Mi who was delighted to see us. A nice government official helping to run the

111

camp asked if I would mind staying until all the old and sick and pregnant women were flown out, and of course we were only too pleased to stay. You children helped in dishing out plates of curry and rice every day. I remember one day Tim saying to me, "Mummy, do you think the 'Jackanese' are sleeping in my bed in Rangoon?" I thought that they probably were, tho' his bed was a drop-side cot!

After a fortnight we were told to go down to the airfield for a possible lift into Assam, but often refugees went in the morning, but were back in the evening as the planes were so busy taking out wounded soldiers. However, we sat round waiting patiently, and then a nasty-looking plane circled round. We thought it was probably a Jap plane, and they were in the habit of swooping down and machine-gunning anybody, so, although it was a boiling hot day, I said to you children, "Let's play a game of tag round that heap of stones," thinking that at least we would not all get hit. I can remember Rachel looking at me with scorn and saying, "Mummy, you must be mad, in this heat!" However, it was one of our own small fighter planes, and we rushed across to see it land.

By the evening we were lined up with our small bundles, hopefully waiting for a returning plane, when we spotted some of our nice soldiers from Maymyo. I remember one of them coming over to see us, and being shocked that after a month from our last meeting we were still in the country. We asked after Pop and were glad to hear that at that time he was still well. I remember thinking of the 121st Psalm as we looked longingly towards the hills – "I will lift up my eyes . . ." Naturally the wounded had to be got away first, but later that day a plane came back over the mountains, and we were lined up again, and told that we could take only a small amount of personal possessions. Do you remember being dressed in everything that you could wear and protesting at the heat? And then the official on the airport saying that you couldn't carry out your Beatrix Potter books or your dolls? However, after my saying, "Oh, you wouldn't part a mother from her child, would you?" he allowed the dolls and a teddy bear. We found that the plane had had all its seats taken out to make enough room for all of us. There were a few benches round the edge, but most people had to sit on their small bundles on the floor of the plane. The plane was loaded down so much that it had difficulty in skimming the tops of those large mountains, but I was not troubled, thinking that the pilot was a well-trained American, until after an hour of this mountain hopping a small Chinese face appeared at the cockpit door and said, "Is you all all-lite?" Then I discovered that *he* was our pilot! I wasn't quite so happy after that; however, we landed safely on a tea estate in Assam, and then were packed into lorries and driven a few miles into Dibrugarh. We arrived at a Roman Catholic church where kind ladies gave us food and blankets, and soon we were all cosily asleep on the hard church floor. At midnight, the nice Salvation Army wife, who had travelled with us, shook my arm and whispered in my ear, "Be careful, there's a man at your feet. He's probably going to steal your money." I lay still and looked at him in the dusk and began to laugh, and whispered to her, "It's all right, it's a statue of St Joseph!"

The next day we were taken down to the Brahmaputra river and loaded on to large river steamers. So many refugees had passed that way already, and the steamers were dirty with no accommodation, so that again we slept side by side on the decks, and ate cold and rather horrible curry and rice on filthy plates. Some kindly English Burma police were with us and whenever the boat tied up to the banks would slip ashore and bring back fruit for us. In two days we reached Tezpur, and again found kind ladies from the tea estates waiting to give us a meal and a bath – bliss indeed!

From there we went in a funny little train with open trucks which fascinated Tim, until we got to a railway junction where we had to wait on the station for some hours for another train to take us to Calcutta. Here the dirt of the steamer, and the filth of the station, caught up with poor Mig who went down with dysentery. There were no lavatories on the station, or only filthy ones, so she and I chased down the line and out to the fields every

113

ten minutes or so – poor Mig, she was so good and patient.

After some hours a train came in and fortunately we found a carriage, packed with refugees of course, but it had a lavatory at the end of the corridor. The journey to Calcutta took some hours, and when we arrived the Army met us and wanted to put us all into some barracks, but I protested and rang up the Bishop, Foss Westcott, and asked if he could advise me what to do as Margaret by this time was very ill. He immediately rang the Oxford Mission sisters, and by the time we reached them in a taxi they had beds prepared and a doctor called, and in two days Mig was well again. How good they were.

Then came the long wait to find out when or if Pop would be out of Burma. This news came within a week, as he had been picked up on Myitkyina airfield, unable to walk, and a lone plane came down and took him over to Dibrugarh, where he had to stay in hospital for over a week. When he finally arrived in Calcutta he was not of course allowed to stay with us at the Sisters, which puzzled you children, but he stayed with the Oxford Mission Fathers and came over every day to see us, until a kindly businessman heard about us and took us along to his palatial house until we could decide what next to do.

The first thing was to find a school for you three – for six months you had had no teaching, except what I could give you, and then kind Miss Budden, the headmistress at Auckland House school, Simla, said she could take you if I could come too and help her nurse about twenty children down with measles in the san., because Matron was coping with some children with suspected diphtheria in another block. So off we went, leaving Pop at "Prospect Lodge" in Simla (a holiday home for missionaries) until he was asked to go down to Poona and look after a soldiers' club. I stayed until the measles epidemic was over, a matter of a few weeks, and then joined him with Tim in Poona. It was horrid leaving you two girls in Simla, but within a few weeks – at the end of that term – we were able to have you down with us in Poona, and you went to the Wantage Sisters' school there, and Tim went too.

Pop and I had never had much to do with a soldiers' club – except for that brief time in Maymyo, which was more of a hospital than a club, but now we had to feed and house soldiers on leave, poor men who were tired and bored and away from their families. I think you children were a delight to them and they would gather round the swimming pool and cheer you on with swimming lessons. We ran a Monday night dance for them, but sometimes they got drunk and would chase each other through the club, and one night one of them fell into the swimming pool and climbed up the stairs to sit on the end of Rachel's bed! I can see him now, and you three children comforting him because he had left his family in England! But I was a bit apprehensive!

After six months Pop was asked to return to Simla to help the Burma Governor, Dorman-Smith, as Director of Public Relations, and to help the Administration and the Army who were by this time getting ready to go back into Burma. People like General Orde Wingate were training men, one of whom was David Patterson, one of our clergy, and Pop helped by writing a book on Burmese for them in case they got separated from their units. He travelled a lot in India at that time, talking to troops and meeting leaders, and so met many interesting people.

While we were in Poona we bought darling Sally because Rachel had become rather afraid of dogs, and while we were there who should turn up one day but dear old Madriya – he had come out of Burma on foot with his wife and daughter – he carried my old sewing machine for some time! Then his wife died on the trek and he and his daughter walked into India and asked people everywhere – Did they know where Padre Appleton was? until at last he tracked us down to Poona. Bless his faithful old heart! I think about five thousand died on that trek. We took him with us to Simla, and what a blessing he was.

Do you remember Padam Cottage on "Jacko Hill", and later moving down to Christ Church Lodge near to the dear Claydons? What fun you children had skating on the tennis courts down in the valley, and putting on plays and dances with the Claydons.

I hope they remember too. I remember Elizabeth Thursfield with John Richard and Anthony, waiting anxiously for Rupert to come out of Burma, and John Richard coming down to have lessons with me.

Do you remember those lovely Himalayas with snow on them in the distance, the picnics out to Wildflower Hall (Lord Kitchener's old residence), the horrible rock pythons twined round an Indian's neck (they were harmless), the lepers that bothered Rachel, and the teas at Davico's? Then Sally's lovely nine puppies – I remember you waylaying an army captain to let Sally mate with his dog, and he ringing us up laughing and saying of course he could, and you three making a lovely bridal room for them in Pop's study!

Then the nice soldiers on leave who came to stay with us – and silly but nice old Narodo, our second bearer, who always forgot to give us plates at meals?

Tim falling down the Kud and brought in by a kind Indian, unconscious for a day, and in hospital for a week.

Tim going to school with his arms round a nice Indian boy's neck.

Mig in hospital with horrible jaundice, me in the next room with suspected typhoid – but it wasn't! Both of us taken down to hospital in a kind of litter – there were no cars in Simla, only rickshaws.

All the nice Burma people attached to Government who lived in Simla, and were so kind to us, who opened a room on the top of the library just below our house for soldiers on leave. Margaret Brewitt ran it (old Burma Railways).

I remember going to Government House with Pop to lunch with the Wavells who had divided their house for wounded and men on leave, and had heard of our soldiers in Maymyo and in Poona.

Do you remember the Mall – that large expanse at the top of the Ridge, where Kipling must have walked and written his Just So stories?

Then back to England at the end of the war, waiting in Bombay for the boat, no black out this time! Malvern, and you and Mig going to "Ellerslie" and Tim to Colwall. Pop having to return to Burma for another year with the Governor, and finally my going to meet him in Liverpool when he was sent home at the end of that year very sick, never to return to Burma.

But you know the rest – this is just a tribute to three lovely unselfish children, and it may bring back some lovely memories, as it does to Pop and myself. Bless you!

CHAPTER 11

Suburban Holiness

M y return to England at the end of 1946, brought about by a severe period of amoebic dysentery together with family responsibilities, raised the pressing question of future work. SPG with their usual generous understanding of the needs of their missionaries were ready to grant whatever furlough was necessary. Two possibilities were suggested: the first a secretaryship in a big ecumenical publishing society and the second a parish in the London diocese. The first offered double the stipend of the second, plus the prospect of a generous pension, but this raised in my mind a cautious signal that the material remuneration was too big a factor in the offer. So on 25th March 1947 I was inducted to the living of St George's, Headstone, a parish at the foot of the hill in Harrow occupied by the famous public school.

The parish was solidly middle class with many parishioners working in posts of responsibility in firms and organisations, though hardly any of them at the directorial level. There were about nine thousand people in the parish, mostly living in their own houses, or houses being bought on mortgage. They had a good churchgoing tradition under a vicar who had been there for twenty-five years who perhaps might have retired earlier, for in his later years he had not been able to go out vigorously into the parish, though both he and the parishioners had accepted the solution that they should come to him rather than he to them. In his earlier years he had organised a system of street wardens who would keep him in touch with newcomers, births, illnesses, deaths, and variations in family fortune. The church, a lovely light building, had been built in 1910, there was a very good modern hall and playing fields for cricket, tennis and other games. There was a very flourishing Mothers Union which seldom had less than eighty to a hundred women attending each monthly meeting, and in addition a Young Wives Fellowship which worked on less formal and perhaps more adventurous lines. Scouts and guides had their own hut, and clubs for different ages gathered in the hall. Two quite effective Sunday schools met on the Sunday afternoon.

The laity were vigorous and resourceful, realising that with the advancing age of their vicar they had to take initiative and responsibility.

I had only been there two weeks when a group of laymen came with the suggestion that on Sunday nights we should study a series of what they called "Vital Questions," including such topics as "Why do we believe in God?", "What is God like?", "Why go to church?", "Why Pray?". "Why is the church necessary?", "What is the good life?". The suggestion was mutually acceptable. Invitation cards were printed and given out to every house. On each of the Sunday nights earmarked for this purpose I attempted my own answers to these questions and after the evening service we adjourned to the hall for general discussion, which on every occasion went on in an animated way for well over an hour. There were several critical parishioners who needed to be convinced about the answers given in church and who on the whole were eager to be convinced.

Later in my short time at Headstone someone in each street gave a little At Home in which neighbours were invited to "meet the vicar" over coffee and refreshments. These very enjoyable evenings were followed a few months later by invitations to the guests to meet my wife and myself in the vicarage. The idea was to get on friendly terms and to understand what people really hoped for from their parish priest.

Congregations were good both morning and evening and the collections were quite generous. But there was a need for more systematic giving so that the work of the parish could be extended as well as its support for charitable causes and work overseas. So a freewill offering scheme was suggested. This came in for a great deal of suspicion and reluctance, and it was only after some weeks that I discovered the real reason. People did not want their neighbours to know too much about their financial position, and I sensed that it was not because they were unwilling to give but because in many cases their salaries were not very high and they would tend to be a little ashamed of the amount they could set apart for support of their church. When it became clear that the pledged amounts would be known only to the vicar and that the secretary and treasurer of the fund would only know the numbers allocated to people, suspicion was allayed. The result was that within a year the income of the parish was practically doubled. Normal collections were abandoned, though there was always the opportunity for visitors or non-subscribers to put something into the bag at the back of the church. It was interesting to note that some indication of the regularity of churchgoing could be deduced by the number of envelopes of the same number on occasional Sundays. People were also glad to be assured that if there was any sudden change in their circumstances they were free to revise their weekly amount. Gradually we moved towards the acceptance of the principle that we should love our neighbour as ourselves by aiming to give half of our church income to people or causes outside the parish.

St George's was the only place of worship in the parish, and this had been assumed to be a considerable advantage. I was not quite so sure of this, for I had been involved in ecumenical relationships overseas. After a while we agreed to approach the minister and people of the Methodist church just outside the parish. Pulpits were exchanged and finally a small meeting of representatives from each denomination was arranged in which the two ministers were allowed to be present but not to speak; all the speaking was to be undertaken by the lay folk. The Methodists won the toss and batted first, each of the four representatives giving some estimate of what his own church meant to him and what that church was trying to do for the world. My four parishioners were keenly interested in what they heard from the Methodists and I became a little anxious lest they should want to change their denomination. However things were evened out when the four Anglicans gave their assessment. Afterwards the Methodist minister confided in me that he had become quite anxious lest he should be losing four of his stalwarts to us Anglicans. Reflection on the evening made it clear that both parties were thrilled to find the other speaking much the same language, sharing a common faith, with the same ideals of personal life and a similar concern for people outside, both at home and abroad.

Towards the end of my second year in Headstone the Bishop of London called all his 600 parishes to co-operate in a mission to the whole city. Preparatory studies were undertaken, attempts were made to deepen the devotional life and a very big advertising firm was engaged to give the diocese some idea of how to commend the Christian truths, though the advertising experts were very insistent that they alone could not do the job, which had to be backed up by solid work in the churches. One particular technique which the advertising firm gave us was the need for every parish to have a correspondent for the local paper and to send in news regularly every week. This not only kept people informed, but the developing feature in the local papers was noticed by the national press and so the mission got much wider attention. Parishes joined together for the week of mission and there were meetings each evening of the week with combined services on the two Sundays. Afterwards the bishop asked for careful assessment of the effects of the mission. St George's was at first rather disappointed because some felt that we had not drawn in many additional people. Gradually it dawned on us that we had been working very much on a mission basis before the Mission was planned. Quite a number of people had been drawn in already and the result of the Mission was that they were confirmed in faith and discipline. Thirty years later I still occasionally meet people who look back on that Mission as the time when they were clinched into Christian loyalty and service.

There was always a good attendance at the eight o'clock

celebration of Holy Communion on Sundays, and before long I introduced a very short address. This lasted only three minutes at the longest and consisted of one single thought drawn from the collect or epistle or gospel for the day. At the farewell party when I left the parish, the churchwarden who made the main speech of thanks said he was quite sure that the best thing that I had done in my time there was this short weekly point at the Sunday Communion. I have tried to keep up the practice ever since.

CHAPTER 12

Widening Vision

I had been vicar of St George's for less than three years, when the Chairman and Senior Secretary of the Conference of British Missionary Societies approached me to become one of their Associate Secretaries. After careful prayer and thought I declined this invitation. Several months later they approached me again and informed me that they had kept the vacant post open as they still felt that I was the right man for the job. Circumstances had changed somewhat and it now seemed right to accept the pressing call. So from the beginning of 1950 I became an ecumenical missionary secretary, with headquarters at Edinburgh House near Sloane Square. No house was provided, but the diocese of London allowed me to use a vacant vicarage at St Michael's Cricklewood. In return I was to be responsible for weekend services.

Edinburgh House had been named after the great missionary Conference at Edinburgh in 1910. It was to be the home of the International Missionary Council in preparation, as well as the centre for co-operation of the missionary societies and boards of Great Britain, with the title of the Conference of British Missionary Societies (CBMS).

The continuation committee of the Edinburgh Conference defined the functions of the planned International Missionary Council as being to stimulate thinking and investigation in missionary questions, to make the results available for all missionary societies and missions, to help to co-ordinate the activities of the national missionary organisations of the different countries and of the societies they represent, to help unite Christian public opinion in support of freedom of conscience and religion and of missionary liberty, to help unite the Christian forces of the world

123

in seeking justice in international and inter-racial relations.

I found these overarching aims and functions both imperative and inspiring. In my twenty years in Burma I had been trying to put them into practice in the Burma Christian Council, of which I had been Secretary and later Chairman.

Almost the first thing I was asked to do on joining the staff of Edinburgh House was to visit the headquarters of the member societies. One of the visits I remember most vividly and gratefully was that to the Methodist Missionary Society, where the Senior Secretary advised me not to feel I had to say something about every question raised in the various committees, but to listen to the questions raised and opinions expressed and to seek a common mind and acceptable decision. Another remembered visit was to the overseas headquarters of the Church of Scotland, where I soon received a stern warning about using the word "English", when I ought to speak of "British".

My main responsibility at Edinburgh House was in the home relationships of the member societies and in the encouragement of the production of Christian literature overseas. Fortunately a colleague had been working for some years in the care of vernacular literature in Africa, so I was able to concentrate on Asia, with special attention to the needs of Burma.

One of the most important features of the year's programme was the annual conference of the CBMS at Swanwick, at which the question of intercommunion was a sensitive one, with two of the three main Anglican societies being strongly opposed, though eager to have a separate Eucharist for Anglicans which others might attend if they wished. In the early years of the fifties I was responsible for these annual conferences, and felt very keenly the tensions aroused and the pain of not yet being ready to share the deepest spiritual level of worship and unity.

After two years at Edinburgh House it was decided that I should undertake a four months' tour, to enquire into the needs of vernacular Christian literature and also to enlarge my knowledge of the Churches' missionary activities. In the course of this journey I spent five days in Cairo, five days in Persia, a week in

Pakistan, eight weeks in India, a fortnight in Burma, two days only in Ceylon, ten days in Singapore and three weeks on the journey back through Africa visiting key people in Kenya, Northern Rhodesia, Nigeria and the Gold Coast, the names of those four countries being those used at that time. Looking back from over thirty years later I shall try to mention insights and highlights perceived.

In Egypt I found that out of a population of twenty million, over a million were Coptic Christians, 70,000 more Copts were members of the Roman Catholic Church, 50,000 Greek Orthodox, and 70,000 Evangelical Christians were under the care of the American Mission. There were less than 2,000 Anglicans, who tried to be on friendly terms with the other bodies.

I remember visiting the CMS hospital in old Cairo, and being deeply impressed with two large open-air wards where up to four hundred people camped out and were fed and given courses of treatment for foot-worms and bilharzia. I got to know a retired government officer, Mr Habib Said, who organised the translation of short English books. He was generously supported by SPCK.

At the time of my visit the welfare state was being set up in Britain, and thoughtful Egyptian Christians inquired how it was being paid for; on being told that it was financed by taxation, in which wealthy people were required to pay a bigger sum than poorer people, listeners were doubtful whether that would be possible (at that time) in Egypt. Literacy teaching was undertaken by Christian workers and I was told that one of the very few Christian landowners had been heard to remark, "For God's sake don't teach my peasants to read, otherwise they will give trouble!" There was dreadful poverty in Egypt and still is, with people living in the tombs in a large area reserved for the burial of the dead.

From Cairo, in company with Dr Alfred Moore, who was the right-hand man of Dr Frank Laubach, the American apostle of literacy, we flew on to Teheran and were warmly welcomed by Bishop Thompson, who arranged an exhilarating literature conference. The Anglican Church in Iran was a very small body,

125

emphasising medical and literature work. It was on that short visit that I first met Hassan Dehqani-Tafti who had been set apart for literature work. He had a splendid knowledge and love of Persian poetry. He and Bishop Thompson's daughter Margaret fell in love and together have done a splendid task in caring for Iranian people in many countries and suffered much for the cause of Christ. When his father-in-law retired, Hassan became Bishop, and is now in exile from his beloved country. To the great grief of Hassan and Margaret their son was assassinated in the revolution, and their forgiving spirit has moved all who have got to know them. I count them as among my dearest friends, and was thankful that Hassan was elected President-Bishop of the Anglican province of Jerusalem and the Middle East.

In Pakistan Dr Moore and I were both struck with the enthusiasm for the new state. Zafrullah Khan was its Foreign Minister, and declared that Islam as a missionary religion should therefore be prepared to allow freedom to Christianity, a similar missionary religion. We were told that the Pakistan government was eager to have all the help that the Christian Church could give in educational, medical and welfare work.

The eight weeks spent in India were a great joy, for at that time the Burma Christian Council was a member of the India National Christian Council which embraced the national councils of India, Pakistan, Burma and Ceylon, and the diocese of Rangoon was under the Metropolitan of Calcutta. In both of these relationships I had had a happy and inspiring association. It is almost impossible to summarise the visit there and to do justice to the outstanding leaders I was privileged to meet, both indigenous and missionary.

The love of the missionary staff, both men and women, for their people was very obvious. The Churches were trying to set a pattern of devotion and skill in their agricultural missions, printing presses, bookshops, village schools, central high schools, medical training colleges, and in some cases the joint training of ordinands, all with their sights on a strong indigenous Church which could accept responsibility for leadership in the care of its

126

own members, and service to others as well, in the different language regions.

I was very thrilled with my visit to the Henry Martyn School of Islamic Studies at Aligarh with its sympathetic examination of Muslim theological terms and its aim of expressing Christian beliefs in terms understandable to Muslims. The staff there were disappointed in the use which Christian missions made of their work. Were they able to know of later developments they would see that they were undertaking a pioneer sowing of seed which only needed time to germinate.

In Calcutta the YMCA Publishing House were producing two splendid series, *The Heritage of India* and *The Religious Life of India*, the latter being originally edited for the Oxford University Press.

South India had developed Christian work over a longer history with its small Church traditionally stretching back to apostolic times. Its literature work was carried on by workers from the CLS of London, building up a strong publishing centre under the organising skill of Mr W.H. Warren. Parallel with this British initiative was the work of an American expert, Miss Ruth Ure. I was able to get to know both, and thought I perceived a romance developing, which verified my perception in their marriage.

It was in South India that a conviction of the imperative of Christian unity grew up, resulting in the formation of the Church of South India, in which Anglicans, Methodists, Presbyterians and Baptists came together. It took a good deal longer for a similar union in North India to take place.

On this journey of exploration, I was able to be present at an international and inter-racial conference on Christian literature, which took place in Singapore, attended by representatives of the Churches I have just mentioned, and also by delegates from the Philippines, Hong Kong and Japan, which generated the hope of a united Church and a more distant vision of a unity of the human race, with the United Nations Organisation succeeding the earlier League of Nations.

I was particularly impressed with a pioneer effort in Bangalore in the School for the Study of Society, dealing with the principles on which a just order of society can be built. Its secretary, Mr Thampe, was an ex-Communist, now a convinced and enthusiastic Christian, who saw the need for studying the relationship between freedom, social justice and peace.

I admired the enthusiasm of American missionaries for literacy and well remember an afternoon in South India with a missionary who had produced some simple leaflets to explain the Christian gospel. One could tell quickly whether a person could read or not, by the puzzled look on the face of an illiterate villager into whose hands a leaflet had been given.

Christmas 1952 was spent in Burma, mainly in Mandalay, the centre of Burmese history and Buddhist activity which had been almost destroyed in the war. It was a joy to be back among old friends, and I was glad to see the revival of the American Baptist Press in Rangoon and the resumed publication of books and pamphlets both in the vernacular languages and in English.

On my visit to Nigeria later in my tour, it was to be heart-warming to be told by a veteran missionary of over forty years' service that the need of which he was most conscious was a book showing what Christ does in the soul, transforming and empowering, killing selfishness, and making something unique and holy out of very ordinary human material. This need was also stressed by the Literature Conference in Singapore which included in its findings a request for books dealing with the Church's vital concern for social justice, and the need to study the purpose and function of the state, the rights and responsibilities of citizens, the organisation of labour, rival political and economic theories, all considered in the light of the Christian revelation.

From Rangoon I flew to Bombay, and I stayed with the bishop there. On the afternoon when I was booked to fly to East Africa the bishop came to my room where I was packing and told me of the death of King George VI. The next day I arrived in Nairobi, as the new young Queen Elizabeth, with the Duke of Edinburgh, were interrupting their East African tour to fly back to London for their new royal duties.

Christian members of staff in the University of the Gold Coast

The cricket team at St Augustine's Missionary College, Canterbury, *c.* 1925.
George is seated on the right of the front row

Left George and Marjorie on their wedding day in Rangoon Cathedral, 1929.
Right Marjorie with her two daughters, Rachel and Margaret

Students and staff of St Mary's Teacher Training School, Kemmendine, *c.* 1935

George with General Aung San addressing Public Relations Officers in
Rangoon in the late 1940s

The War Memorial Reredos at St George's, Headstone, Harrow, 1948

Margaret, Timothy, George, Marjorie and Rachel on the
vicarage lawn in Harrow, 1950

Left On arrival in Perth, Western Australia, 1963. *Right* With a representative
of the Australian Aborigine community

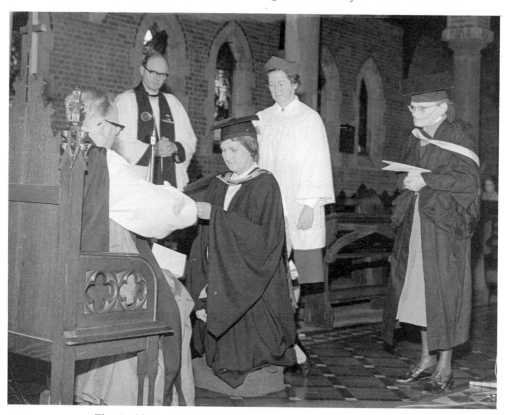

The Archbishop licenses Deaconesses to baptise, preach and
take part in divine worship, 1967

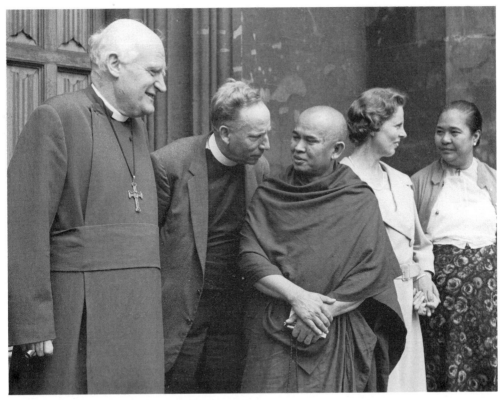

As interpreter between a Burmese monk and Archbishop Michael Ramsey

In Rome with Pope Paul VI, 1968

The new Archbishop in Jerusalem being received by the
President of Israel, 1969

With Archbishop Makarios (centre), 1969

Left Greeting the Armenian patriarch, Yegishe Derderian, 1969.
Right In Beirut, meeting Arab Christians from the Near East Christian Council

With Mayor Teddy Kollek in Jerusalem

George in his early sixties while Archbishop of Perth, Australia (as it was then called) were keen on Christian literature, and ready to take part in providing theological texts, if they could get the leisure to do the writing. So I included in my report to the British Missionary Societies a suggestion that they should approach the theological colleges in Britain to release lecturers for a term to visit theological colleges overseas and relieve personnel to write some of the basic theological books needed. This proposal was gladly implemented. I was also impressed by the interest taken by Gold Coast staff in tribal customs and their plan to see how these could be interpreted in Christian understanding and practice.

On my arrival back in London I reported at some length to the missionary societies on this four months' fact-finding and exploratory tour. One of the things that I had discovered in the many "Christian" bookshops was that their local income came almost entirely from the sale of stationery and government pamphlets. In their printing activities there was a need for modern presses, they needed capital loans to replace old machines and to enable bigger editions of basic religious literature.

Books for clergy and teachers were needed to help them in their tasks. One of the most fruitful developments was a plan for a series of World Christian Books, simply written and then translated into vernaculars by indigenous scholars who thought and wrote in their own languages. An inspired suggestion came from Canon Max Warren, the General Secretary of the Church Missionary Society and a great missionary statesman. His suggestion was that Bishop Stephen Neill should be invited to organise this. He was at the time recovering from a psychological illness and looking round for an activity in which to employ his great gifts of the languages of South India, his concern for the clergy of all denominations and his pastoral experience as a bishop.

Stephen happily accepted the call, the missionary societies of America and Britain provided the necessary finance and the scheme was launched. The bishop quickly recruited skilled and trusted writers and raised money for overseas translation and publishing. Max commended the plan in his monthly CMS Newsletter and a fund was raised to cover the early volumes.

Stephen could have written every basic book himself, but he humbly and generously counselled the writers and translators, and when the number of translations reached five hundred, a dinner of commemoration was held in the House of Lords in London. In the same period Stephen recruited two associate editors to whom he finally handed over the editorship.

Another development inherent in the experience and insights of this journey of discovery was a plan to recruit short-term workers to serve in the needs I have mentioned. An imaginative plan to recruit these workers was organised in conjunction with the Student Christian Movement, under the title of "53 Scheme", the hope being to enlist fifty-three workers during the year 1953. It transpired in consultation that the overseas colleges and hospitals would pay the same salary as they did to their own nationals, if the fares from the sending missions could be borne, together with a modest grant for clothing and a promise that their fares back would be made available by agreement with the sending and receiving bodies. The full target of fifty-three recruits was not reached in 1953, but it was achieved a year or two later.

The two great Bible Societies, the British and Foreign Bible Society and the American Bible Society, offered their facilities in Bible translation and publishing. A fascinating book written by Eugene A. Nida, entitled *Bible Translation*, published by the American partner, still affords inspiration and practical wisdom to all engaged in Christian literature work.

Looking back over forty years since I was sent on this journey, I see how the British churches and missionary societies were eager to pool their experiences and offer their contributions in service and money once they became aware of the needs and op-portunities.

Two further memories of my time at Edinburgh House still excite me. The first concerns the Secretary of what was known then as the Mission to Lepers. He told me that for many years he and the members had been praying that they might be allowed to open up work in Nepal. Permission had now been given by the Nepalese government, on the condition that there should be no public preaching of the Christian message. He said that his Council had refused to accept this ruling. He asked if I felt that this decision was a right one. It soon dawned on me that he was rather troubled about it. I found myself saying that their caring hands would do the preaching more eloquently than any words. My friend Donald Miller took this thought back to his Council, which then reversed their initial decision. A year or two later, when I enquired about the progress of the leprosy work, he reported that there were now several hunded Nepalese Christians who were free to bear their witness, whereas the white missionaries were regarded with suspicion as foreigners with a political virus.

The final mention in this chapter must be the widely expressed desire for help in prayer and meditation. That stuck in my mind and nagged at the spirit. I came to see that I needed a discipline of intercession and meditation for my own devotional life. So when the International Missionary Council held a great conference in July 1952 at Willengen in Germany and expressed a need similar to my own, I felt emboldened to offer to prepare a cycle of prayers and biddings with the Scriptural insights which inspired them. The offer was warmly welcomed and after three years of wide consultation and co-operation, under the critical guidance of Miss Phyllis Hocken, editor of the Edinburgh House Press, *In His Name* was published with the sub-title of *Prayers for the Church and the World*. I still use this anthology myself, and would make only one correction. I would now put "for the World and the Church", in accordance with the New Testament statement that "God so loved the world . . .", putting the world before the Church.

CHAPTER 13

Unexpected Friends

A s my time at Edinburgh House moved into its eighth year I began to feel that a change was necessary. I felt rather frustrated in trying to organise other people, with a growing desire to get back into pastoral work. Another theme was growing in strength, namely that to influence one's own Church in world mission one had to be actively within it. From my early days in this ecumenical post I had felt that the Church of England rather regarded its people engaged in it not as representatives who could be advised or consulted, but as almost being outside the important work of the Church. Also I found my mind working towards fairly definite conclusions about the attitude of Christians to other faiths, and I wanted to be rather more free to pursue this interest than seemed possible in the circumstances of the missionary societies. There was a deeper personal reason – I found myself becoming too secretarial and somewhat bureaucratic, raising appropriate questions in committees and adopting a growingly stereotyped response to the routine business of the Conference. So a change seemed necessary.

It came in an unexpected way. I had come to know an Anglican priest who had been born in Eastern Europe in a Jewish family. He had ultimately come to England where he became a Christian and finally was ordained in the Anglican Church. He had been approached about the possibility of becoming rector of St Botolph's Church, Aldgate, the most easterly parish of the City churches. He wanted advice about the spiritual possibilities in such a parish where almost all the parishioners were Jews. I gave him my own vision of the opportunity to build a new relationship between Christians and Jews, not as an evangelistic exercise, but as an experiment in mutual understanding and possible joint service in community needs. In due time he was interviewed by the churchwardens who decided that in their view he was not a suitable priest for St Botolph's. The Bishop of Stepney, Bishop Joost de Blank, who had been the vicar of a neighbouring parish to mine in Harrow, then came to me and suggested that in the light of what I had told my friend, I was the one person for Aldgate.

Shortly afterwards I went to meet the churchwardens, one a rather stiff lawyer and the other the head of the Whitechapel bell foundry. After the opening skirmishes they said to me, "This parish will not take up all the time of a man as active as you seem to have been. What additional interest would you take up?" I replied that I was deeply interested in contacts between people of different faiths, and I would like to make St Botolph's a centre for new relationships. Then came the vital question, "With Jews?" and with a feeling of rash abandon I answered, "Not with Jews only but with Buddhists, Hindus and Muslims as well", rather expecting that this reply would bring the interview to a speedy end. To my surprise they reacted with enthusiasm, saying that they did not want a man who would make an aggressive approach to Jews, but they would welcome one who had the all-round approach that my last remark had indicated.

Their acceptance was reported to the Bishop of Stepney, who was overjoyed and promised that if I accepted the offer of the living the diocese would appoint me as secretary of the London Mission to Jews with a grant of four hundred pounds a year which I could use towards the salary of a curate. The Bishop of London, Bishop Wand, quickly approved and asked me to become rector almost at once, though being willing that I should continue as General Secretary of the Conference of British Missionary Societies until they were ready to name a successor. Fortunately this lasted only two further months. There was one rather pressing problem in that there was no rectory, for my predecessor had begun his incumbency at a time when it was not thought necessary for City clergy to live within the City, but to commute on a number of days a week. This seemed to me altogether unsatisfactory, and fortunately an old friend from Selwyn days came to the rescue. Basil Jansz was vicar of Shadwell and had a very large rectory, the top floor of which was not in use. The diocese agreed to make it habitable, and the capital expended was to be recouped out of the modest rent that I was asked to pay. Shortly before Christmas 1958 we moved to east London, and on 1st January I became full-time rector.

One of the first things that I was able to do, with the Bishop's permission, was to invite all my old colleagues from the missionary societies to come to St Botolph's one morning for a corporate Communion and friendly breakfast. All through my years at Edinburgh House I had been troubled by the fact that several Anglican missionary societies did not feel that any inter-communion was yet acceptable, either at conferences or in visits to the missionary headquarters of other Churches. Now that I was a free agent I was glad to be able to invite the people with whom I had worked in a happy co-operation to join in the deepest act of spiritual fellowship. Some of my Anglican ex-colleagues from Edinburgh House were not too happy with this invitation, but they came, and we prayed together for wisdom and grace for their former colleague in this new venture.

I received a very warm welcome from two fellow incumbents of City churches with whom I had become friendly in my ecumenical missionary secretaryship. The first was the Reverend Norman Motley, rector of St Michael's Cornhill, a lovely Wren church. He had served as a chaplain in the RAF during the war, and had returned to parochial life determined to work for spiritual and social principles which would make further war unnecessary. With this vision he founded two communities, on the lines of the Iona Community, the first at Bradwell-on-Sea in Essex, where with financial co-operation from friends in the City he was able to secure 500 acres of farmland at a bargain price near a dilapidated Saxon chapel which became the centre for a whole series of weekly conferences, partly holiday and partly community life, largely of younger people, camping out and doing all their own work. He named this experiment in community living after the Saxon name of the region, Othona. While still an ecumenical missionary worker I was invited by Norman to be responsible for one of the weeks. The second experiment was a rather less Spartan effort, where his keen community spirit learnt of a complete community settlement, at Burton Bradstock near Bridport in Dorset, coming to an end, and after negotiations it was handed over to him and given the name of Othona Community Centre. Its programme was much on the lines of the Essex Othona. Norman's work in St Michael's and in the two community centres was greatly encouraged by Archbishop Fisher.

The other City rector whose parish bordered on Aldgate was the world-famous Tubby Clayton, who had come through the First World War with the vision which inspired Toc H. He had made his headquarters in a lovely old house in Trinity Square, which had been formerly the home of rectors of St Botolph's. The three of us were regular attendants at the monthly meeting of the City Chapter. When Father Joe Williamson became rector of an East End neighbouring parish and built up his rescue work among women involved in prostitution we four priests worked together, prayed together, and encouraged each other's responsibilities. Norman Motley's responsibility was a heavy one, for he had developed a heart condition which was liable to be fatal and in the end was so. His two communities of Othona are still in active operation under the leadership of his much-loved daughter Janet.

I am the only one of the four ageing musketeers who has survived, and I remember with affection and gratitude the fellowship and encouragement that I received from the three now promoted to the spiritual and eternal sphere.

Aldgate was not a parish in the conventional sense of the word. There were about a thousand people actually living in it but in the daytime a score or more thousands of workers came in from outside. Of the thousand permanent residents 950 were Jews and of the remaining fifty there were only two or three faithful Anglicans, so it was clear that the rector should have some friendly, and if possible pastoral, relationship with Jews who were

135

either residents or working within the parish. I did a fair amount of visiting, but it was the Jews who helped me to see a new relationship. From time to time a Jew would drop into the church, where I more or less sat for the working hours of the week, sometimes a man grieved at the death of his wife, once or twice parents who were worried that their son or daughter had fallen in love with a Christian, occasionally people concerned about a son or a daughter who was in trouble with drink or drugs or bad companions. One such Jewish visitor said to me, "You Anglicans believe that the parish priest has some responsibility for everyone living in the parish. You are our rector, so we want your comfort and advice from time to time, particularly if you do not press us to abandon our Jewish faith and culture." This remark gave me a completely new vision of pastoral opportunity, for I could now see that if Christian clergy were prepared to be friendly and pastoral without any conditions or ulterior motives, the Christian Church could become a pastoral community provided it did not insist on claiming this responsibility or exploiting it. The insight gained in this way has been of great practical value in the years since that conversation.

At the end of the first year we were able to have a course of mid-week talks from Jewish rabbis, who spoke to us about their own understanding of the "Torah", the Law of the Lord, their understanding of the prophets and the later writings of the Jewish Bible and the Jewish attitude to morality and charitable service. In the diocesan committee for Jewish work, of which I was now the secretary, we soon began to discuss the need of a new way of working and a new name. Finally we settled on the name London Diocesan Council for Christian-Jewish Understanding. The next step was to ask the Dean and Chapter of St Paul's if we could inaugurate an annual lecture in the cathedral which would be given in alternate years by Jewish and Christian scholars. This proposal was gladly accepted and the first lecture in the crypt of St Paul's was given by Dr Leon Roth on "Foundations", an exposition as challenging and satisfying to Christians as to Jews. The lecture has continued annually. The audiences have not been large, but as the lecture was always published by the CCJU every year, it reached quite a wide public. Perhaps the biggest audience gathered together was for the lecture given in 1976 by the Chief Rabbi on the subject of "Jewish Medical Ethics". Well over a hundred people attended, and the lecture was given by Dr Jacobovitz in the chapel of the Order of the British Empire, a gracious gesture of courtesy on his part, for previously the lectures had been given in a part of the crypt not reserved for Christian worship.

Aldgate was not only on the eastern edge of the City, it was equally the western frontier of Stepney. For generations Stepney had been a place in which "down-and-outs" congregated or where people came who wanted to escape public notice for a time. The coming of a new rector was a joyful opportunity for some of these visitors and in less than no time there was a steady stream every day of mostly men but sometimes women who were hard up for a night's lodging, a meal or, less respectably, a bottle of methylated or surgical spirit. In my earliest years in Stepney as a curate it had often been said that the quickest way out of east London was via three pennyworth of gin. But gin was now too expensive, and ironmongers and chemists were the "off-licence" if a man did not have sufficient money to buy enough beer at one of the many pubs. It soon became clear that something needed to be done by way of friendly service, and we looked at the crypt of the church, which consisted of little more than three round tunnels for storage of fuel, unwanted furniture or things that we wanted hidden away. We cleared out most of the accumulated relics of the past, whitewashed the tunnels, put in electric light and what the men needed most of all, wash basins, lavatories and a bath. The work was carried out by a one-man contractor from Kingston who became so interested in the project that he offered to come and run a club for the old boys if I could raise enough money to keep him and pay for his season ticket. Somehow we managed to do this and Harry King duly took over as warden of a daily club. Every evening we tried to provide a meal, but before long had to ration the number of guests each night, or when we

137

had had a generous gift provide a second sitting. Occasionally there would be no money and no food, and then one of the men would go out to the markets to secure meat or fish or vegetables or fruit which was getting beyond saleable possibility. The meal most nights was a huge hotpot, though occasionally we rose to fish and chips, sometimes even purchased from a local fish and chip shop.

The churchyard had become a haunt for meths drinkers, and this continued after the opening of the Crypt Club, for the men were loyal to our only rule that no drink was to be brought into the crypt, except that provided by the management, which on festive occasions when cash was available consisted of good wholesome beer.

The churchyard however remained unredeemed. On one occasion I went out to talk to some of the surreptitious drinkers and found a woman friend of theirs quickly hiding a big bottle of meths under her skirts. I expressed my feelings about this somewhat pointedly. Afterwards one of the men, Oswald, came to me and said that he thought I had been rather unfair in tearing strips off Jessie, for she was a good woman and a special friend of his. I kept my eye on Oswald and Jessie and noted their developing friendship, until one day I asked Oswald why he didn't marry her. The reply was quite conclusive – both of them were already married but their partners had left them. I mooted the possibility of divorce, but this was considered quite impractical, for the partners had completely disappeared, and in any case, the private lives of Oswald and Jessie would not be viewed with great understanding in the divorce court, even if the necessary legal fees could be paid. Neither of them had a home and like most of the others they slept under railway arches or in bombed buildings or occasionally, when money and some abstinence from meths allowed, in the Salvation Army Hostel several hundred yards away from the church. In the end the only happy solution seemed to be that Oswald and Jessie should live "in sin", with the acquiescence of the rector of Aldgate who was able to provide a relatively small sum to rent a room. Oswald and Jessie began to make a home, a pretty miserable dark place with an outside lavatory used by other people in similar circumstances. I was proudly invited to visit them and tea with cakes was provided.

Then came tragedy, for Oswald got mixed up in some escapade of theft and was sentenced to six months' imprisonment. He knew he was guilty and before his trial he commissioned me to keep an eye on Jessie while he was away. I received monthly letters from Oswald reminding me of my responsibility, which I was able to fulfil until the last week before he was due for release. Then somehow Jessie disappeared and I knew that we would be in trouble on the Saturday morning if she was not at the church to welcome him back. As late as Friday we could find no trace of Jessie. Then in despair we sent out the men to search the whole of Stepney, and about six o'clock that evening news came that she was in the Aldgate Arms. I dropped everything and went to the pub and found Jessie with at least twenty boon companions in the public bar. I went up to her and whispered, but she refused to accompany me. The whole bar entered into the discussion and Oswald and I were saved by a kindly drunk who remarked in a loud voice, "The Father is a good man, Jessie. Do what he wants." Jessie reluctantly agreed, but as soon as we got outside the pub she whispered, "Father, I'm tiddly, I'll have to take your arm." So Jessie and I walked up Aldgate High Street arm in arm all the way to Wellclose Square where Father Joe Williamson had got his home for unfortunate ladies like Jessie. His women colleagues gladly took Jessie in, she had a much needed bath, was fitted out with fresh clothes and after a good night's sleep was waiting at the church next morning where shortly after eight Oswald turned up, and Jessie's bacon, and mine, was saved.

All the men claimed some denomination of affiliation – the main bodies represented were Romans and Anglicans, Presbyterians came next and then an occasional Methodist. There was Jock, a convinced Roman Catholic, regular at Sunday Mass, for by Sunday he would have recovered from the Friday night indulgence after drawing his National Assistance. He honoured me by always calling me "Father", but on one memorable occasion when he could not get out of me something he wanted, he loudly proclaimed on the steps of the church that I was no real priest, only the priests of his own Church had any validity to him. The next day he came to seek me out in a very penitent mood, for I think he had been reproached by some of our mutual friends. That day at noon there was a weekday celebration of Holy Communion in St Botolph's and Jock joined the small group of worshippers and kneeling at the altar steps he received Communion. For the time being at any rate the ecclesiastical hatchet had been buried.

There was rather a rowdy Scot, an out-of-work seaman, who was always in trouble on Friday nights. On one such night it was reported to me that he was out in Houndsditch shouting at the top of his voice. I went out and found him supported by two friends nearly as inebriated as himself. All three were shouting and singing. I went up to Sandy and said, "What would the Meenister say, Sandy, if he saw you now?" "To hell with the Meenister and you," came the quick reply. But Sandy was ready to be led to the Crypt Club where a quick meal of bread and cheese was able to act as blotting paper to the earlier liquid refreshment.

There was a wonderful camaraderie among the men and a real concern for one another. A middle-aged man always kept his aged mother with him. They stored their few possessions in a bombed building to which they returned every night. One night they had made a fire to make some tea and somehow got burnt to death, the tragedy not being discovered until the next day. There was genuine grief among all members of the club and quite a congregation of tidy and for the moment sober men at the sad little funeral which took place a few days later.

We had only just got going in a very rough way with the Crypt Club when Harry King spoke to me about the number of youngsters roaming round the streets in the evenings and frequently annoying passers-by and getting into trouble with the police. We were only using half the crypt and so decided to try

140

to do something for these young people, most of whom had already been expelled from other clubs in the East End. A grant from a City charity enabled us to open a club for them in the unused tunnel of the crypt. I went to my Jewish friends to ask their help in providing a juke box, cooking stoves and refrigerator with cutlery and crockery, so that we could provide refreshments for midday and evening. Within a very short time we had a membership of over a hundred young people. The only rules were that they should bring no drink into the club, no drugs and no flick-knives, that there should be no quarrelling and that a small weekly subscription must be paid regularly. The young people did not want to be organised or to make use of the games we provided, but every night there were at least fifty of them jiving to the music of the juke box and being quite content with doing little more than mark dancing time in a very small circle around each couple.

I was interested in the way my Jewish friends collected the necessary money. They made no public appeal and they did not want me to contact possible donors. Instead they made a shortish list of people whom they thought would and could help and these were assessed by the organisers, who said that they knew quite well how much each ought to give, with due regard to the circumstances at the time of asking, some of the necessary equipment being given in kind in preference to money.

The acknowledged leader of the youth club was a young giant of whom most of the members were in fear. Harry King and I decided that if we could win this huge lad over, life in the club would become tolerable for everybody. Sammy was constantly in trouble and he and I had long and sometimes vehement conversations about his problems. On one occasion he went to my wife and told her that "The Rev" really meant what he said when he used "bloody", and he had on that evening said that Sammy was a bloody fool. It seemed that with both old and young in the two crypt clubs the use of the word "bloody" was needed if the persons addressed were to be quite clear what was meant. Its use to me was one of communication rather than exasperation, though occasionally a touch of the latter would enter into the dialogue.

One day Sammy came to me and said that he had been picked up by the police for some attempted theft and had been remanded. Before his next appearance in the court at Mansion House he had taken part in a "sit-in" demonstration in Trafalgar Square against the atomic bomb and had had his name taken for refusing to move at the somewhat peremptory demand of the police. I urged on Sammy that it was rather asking for trouble to get involved when he was on remand for the earlier suspicion. His reply was quite decisive as far as Sammy was concerned, and almost convincing to me, "Well, Rev, we can't have that bloody bomb going on all over the place, can we?"

At the end of my time at Aldgate, after I had actually moved to St Paul's Cathedral, the police made a raid on the Crypt Youth Club. The next morning I went to see the Inspector at Bishopsgate and reproached him that he had not come to see me first. He replied almost apologetically that the police had received a tip-off that drugs were being distributed through the members of the club. Then, as if to console me, he said, "We found no drugs, and only one flick-knife and only one French letter." My former colleagues and I felt that the youth club in the crypt was serving its purpose.

I must go back to my earliest conversation with the church-wardens about making St Botolph's a centre for inter-religious friendships. Our relationship with our Jewish friends was warm and personal, but I still kept thinking about how to make a religious contact with people of other faiths. An opportunity soon came which was also rather a shaking challenge. The World Congress of Faiths came to me to ask if their annual service could be held in St Botolph's church, and pressed on me the fact that it had never yet been able to be held under Anglican responsibility. As in earlier years, I was beset by fears of what other people would say. Fortunately my two churchwardens were ready to approve the request. I wanted the service to be one of real fellowship but also one of real religious integrity, with no blurring of differences and with no singing of hymns so vague in their content that anyone might sing them, and I wanted the prayers to be such as people of each faith could pray in their own way within the silence of their own hearts. So the service had no hymns, there were no set prayers but only biddings, biddings of worship, penitence, thankfulness, and intercessions, and passages were read from the various scriptures by members of each particular faith. A particularly moving moment for me was when the Muslim representative went up into the pulpit to read a passage from the Qur'an, and prefaced his reading by the invocation "In the name of the God of Abraham, Isaac, Ishmael and Jacob", which somehow spoke to my heart of the desire of Muslims to be equally regarded as a people of God with Jews and Christians.

We were joined at Sunday morning worship by a group of West Indians who had been lovingly and faithfully cared for by a Franciscan brother, who had adapted two almost derelict houses in Cable Street for their fellowship and refreshment. Father Charles somehow had a feeling that St Botolph's would be a good home for them. I was more than ready for this, but wondered if St Botolph's was the right place and I the right priest for them. The truly holy father's reply was, "You always welcome them, you don't talk down to them, you don't make a special fuss of them, you treat them in the same way as you do your English worshippers." I prayed inwardly that his judgement was as sound as his hope.

I cannot close this exciting chapter without mentioning someone who in a very quiet but independent way made a real contribution to the work at St Botolph's. Trudy Eulenburg was of partly Jewish origin. She had come to this country and become a Christian and finally been accepted as a woman worker. She was not, said the Bishop of Stepney, Evered Lunt, everyone's cup of tea, but she was quite clearly a very good brand of her own. It seemed that St Botolph's was just the place for her and so she came, took a full part in the life of the two clubs, joined with conviction in the friendly approach to Jews and was ready to do any kind of needed work, and still ready to make any needle-sharp criticism of anything about which she felt doubtful. St Botolph's owes her a real debt of gratitude. As I write these memories, Trudy still visits St Botolph's and takes an interest in the great work in the crypt organised so ably by my successor, Father Malcolm Johnson.

In this look-back in memory to the Aldgate days I must not forget the promise of the diocese to finance a curate. It was fulfilled almost immediately by the arrival of the Reverend Nick Earle. He had had a brilliant career as a student at Oxford, gaining first class honours in both Mathematics and Theology. This was followed by an ecumenical studentship at Union Theological Seminary in the USA. Returning to Britain, he had found difficulty in finding a suitable post, and someone had advised him to apply for the vacancy at St Botolph's. He had been trained as a priest by Mervyn Stockwood, later Bishop of Southwark. Soon after his arrival Nick joined in the open-air preaching on Tower Hill, being very critical of the Church. In the preaching at St Botolph's he had an obvious gift of oratory. One Sunday we had one of the old drunks in church, and when Nick repeated a statement he wished to emphasise, Jimmy was heard to say quite audibly, "I 'eard yer the first time." The sidesman on duty hastened to remove him, but fortunately I was sitting near and managed to calm the disturbance. Nick later became the headmaster of Bromsgrove School near Birmingham and after fourteen years there retired to devote himself to writing and pastoral ministry.

CHAPTER 14

The Heart of a City

St Boltolph's Church was the ward church of the Portsoken Ward, the most easterly ward in the City of London, and one which was predominently Jewish. The alderman was Sir Bernard Waley-Cohen, himself a Jew, and five of the six Common Councillors were Jewish also. They were in no way embarrassed or ungenerous in looking to St Botolph's as their ward church which they attended on special City or national occasions.

Shortly after coming to St Botolph's I was approached by the Sheriff-elect, the representative of the City Guilds, who asked me if I would be his chaplain for the year of office. The other sheriff was elected annually by the Common Court Councillors and in due time moved on in seniority towards the honour of Lord Mayor. The duties were not onerous, mainly to be in attendance on the Sheriff on special occasions and also at the banquets given by the Lord Mayor at the Mansion House or Guildhall. Only wealthy men could think of becoming Sheriff or Lord Mayor, for all the expenses of the office had to be borne by the three chief officers themselves. These included lunch for the judges of the Old Bailey on every day during term. As chaplain to the Sheriff and later to the Lord Mayor I was welcome to drop in and share lunch with the judges whenever it was convenient to do so.

One of the duties of a Sheriff's chaplain was to be present when sentence of death was passed on a convicted murderer. At the sentencing he stood just behind the judge and at the end of the sentence of death added the words "And may the Lord have mercy on your soul." I had not realised this duty when I accepted the invitation to become a Sheriff's chaplain, otherwise I might have declined, for I have always been a worker for the abolition

145

of capital punishment. I tried to comfort myself by really trying to pray the words, and also by the thought that nobody could opt out of responsibilities involved in a particular position. Had I not been so pressed for time in the work of St Botolph's I would have asked to go and see the condemned man and try to comfort and strengthen him as he faced an ordeal which no man should be asked to face, either in his own act of murder or in the punishment by society.

Two years later Sir Bernard became Lord Mayor and invited me as the rector of his Ward church to be his chaplain. To be the Christian chaplain to a Jewish Lord Mayor was something I welcomed as a practical experiment in my thinking about the relationship between Christians and Jews. The chaplain was not expected to be the confessor of the Lord Mayor or to offer him spiritual counsel, though occasionally he would be consulted about religious matters. His main duty was to be in attendance with the Lord Major on all great occasions and to say grace before and after banquets. It took some time to think out how this latter duty could be worked out with integrity to the Lord Mayor and loyalty to one's own religious convictions. Ultimately I seemed to be led into making the opening grace a prayer for the occasion, with no direct mention of Christ but with some of Our Lord's words or thoughts, thus in some way expressing his presence. The grace afterwards was easier – a short expression of thanksgiving for the meal and the fellowship together. A few days before writing these words I happened to come across a small bundle of these prayers and graces which had somehow survived my movements round the world. One such occasion was the visit of the Muslim ruler of a North African state. He had asked for a latin grace to start with and had hinted to the Lord Mayor's staff that he did not want anything of too outspoken a Christian nature. Fortunately my son-in-law, Ian Bennett, had read classics at Cambridge and helped me to put into passable Latin the following opening prayer: "O Eternal and All-ruling God, bless our two countries, our friendship and our efforts for justice and peace, and to you be the glory throughout all centuries."

146

The final grace was:

> Praise be to God, Lord of the worlds,
> The Beneficent, the Merciful,
> The Lifegiver, the Provider,
> Our Sovereign and our Lord.

The next morning an aide to the guest of honour rang up the Mansion House to ask from what source the chaplain had found the closing grace of the night before. I could not help feeling a certain amount of quiet satisfaction in answering that these words came almost verbatim out of the Qur'an.

Another grace which has survived in my scraps of paper was for the banquet to the Ruler of Senegal: "O thou Lion of Judah, be thou also the Lion of Africa and burst all the chains that still bind our African brethren, and deliver them from all injustice and fear, into the Kingdom of thy Love."

After the Lord Mayor's procession at the beginning of his year of office, we were all rather tired, and a short heart-lifting grace was needed. I remembered on the spur of the moment

> For every cup and plateful
> God make us truly grateful.

After a short silence of shock there was a relieving burst of laughter.

Sir Bernard took a great interest in these graces, and often before the procession to the High Table, would say with a smile, "What have you got for us tonight?" I had in the early days consulted him about the ways in which I would try to write and pray these graces, and he had generously said that he left it to my sensitivity to adapt them both to the occasion and to his own religious allegiance.

He took a great interest in the welfare work in the crypt of St Botolph's and often enquired about our progress. On one sad day we discovered that we had absolutely no money for the modest evening meal that needed to be provided. The only hope seemed to be the Lord Mayor. Fortunately he was in his office and agreed to receive me "about a rather urgent matter". I opened by asking how his Charity Fund stood, and if it was not in the red could he give me an immediate small grant. He called the officer in charge and asked what the balance was. The officer looked at his book, wrote down a figure and handed it carefully to the Lord Mayor, who remarked, "Yes, we have some money still in hand." Then he asked the official, "What is our customary maximum grant?" The reply was "twenty-five pounds". Sir Bernard turned to me and said with a twinkle, "That is not much use to you in your present emergencies, is it? How much do you hope for?" Taking the proffered cue I replied, "Would a hundred pounds be possible?" He called for the cheque book, signed a cheque and handed it over to me, with the words, "That is the quickest touch I have ever experienced." There was much joy in the crypt when I got back with the news that we were safe for at least a fortnight!

There was one occasion when the chaplain to the Lord Mayor had an opportunity of speaking at some length to the City; this was at the service which preceded the election of the Lord Mayor for the ensuing year, when he was invited to address the Court of Mayor and Aldermen, together with the Livery of the City Companies, in the Guild Church of St Laurence Jewry, which had been restored by the City after its destruction in the bombing of London. I chose as my text for this occasion Psalm 19:10, "More to be desired than gold, sweeter also than honey", and tried to interpret for Christians and Jews something of the Law of the Lord, both in its negative form of the Ten Commandments and also in the positive form of the two great commands, underlined by Jesus and emphasised by contemporary rabbis, ending with a moving paragraph from Herman Wouk's *This is My God:*

If you are a Jew, you will probably find the Lawgiver in the end waiting for you. He will greet you with the smile and the embrace of my grandfather. "What kept you so long?" he will say. And you will sit down to study the Torah together.

148

A few days later I received what was said to be a unanimous resolution from the Court of Common Council, thanking me "for this admirable discourse!" Possibly they said the same every year to their current chaplain.

During my year of office as Lord Mayor's chaplain I was invited to conduct the Good Friday three-hours service at St Paul's Cathedral. One of the most moving moments to me and to the large congregation was when I was able to quote the words of a judge at the Old Bailey a day or two earlier, when after sentencing the accused man to death he had addressed a young woman who stood in the dock also, charged with sheltering him. She was found not guilty, and the judge, addressing her, began with the words, "My dear". I could not help feeling that these two words, uttered in a place more used to condemnation and punishment, were an echo from the first Good Friday, and were God's perennial greeting to his sinful children.

During Eastertide that same year I was asked by the Dean and Chapter of St Paul's to preach a course of sermons on Sunday nights on the theme of "A Christian Approach to other Faiths". After each service the Dean, Walter Matthews, invited me to supper. There were only the two of us and the follow-up of each sermon greatly encouraged me in my search for the activity of God in other faiths. Walter took down from his bookshelves Rudolf Otto's *Religious Essays*, and read me two extracts which have inspired me ever since:

> The stir of new life in the great religions of the East is largely a result, and a highly desirable result too, of Christian missionary endeavour.

> No religion should die before it has had the opportunity of uttering its last and most profound word.

From time to time in our meetings afterwards, he and I would go back to these words, and once I asked him if it were possible to get a second-hand copy of this out-of-print book. He did not think it possible, but added that both of us must try to find me a copy. After his death, his own copy came to me, so now it has a double value, for its enlightening content and for the mutual affection between us.

Not every one at St Paul's had this understanding attitude towards other faiths, and before the last evening of my short course, the canon-in-residence said, "You seem to have been pressing us to become Jews, Hindus, Buddhists in turn. I suppose tonight you will want us to become Muslims!" We enjoyed a quiet vestry laugh together.

At the end of that year, 1961, the chaplain to the Bishop of London rang up to say that the bishop, Robert Stopford, wanted to see me on a rather urgent matter. Would I be free to receive him at the church in an hour's time? He duly arrived and no sooner had he sat down in my study when he said, "I want you to become Archdeacon of London and Canon of St Paul's Cathedral." I was completely taken aback, and he must have perceived my surprise, for he added, "I think you would be able to continue both interest and support for the work you have been trying to do here." It took me several days to reply, but it seemed right to accept, and I was licensed as Archdeacon at Fulham Palace in January 1962, and on St Paul's day, 25th January, was installed as a Canon of St Paul's Cathedral, at a service in which the congregation was swollen by the five hundred children from Sir John Cass school. As I thought of some of the great preachers and predecessors at St Paul's, my heart almost failed. I think I was saved by two lines from Tennyson:

> God grant our greatness may not fail
> By craven fears of being great

words that have helped me on many occasions since.

The Dean and other canons gave me a warm and generous welcome. Bishop Wand had become a canon after resigning as Bishop of London; he had inducted me to the living of Headstone twelve years earlier. He was the best canon of all of us, unfailing in his attendance at the services of St Paul's, devoted to the care of the cathedral which was his special canonical assignment, and never letting the episcopal aura of the past in any way affect his relationships with the other three of us. Canon Frederick Hood was equally devoted and disciplined. In addition he was the confidential father-in-God for clergy all over England who were under discipline for varying causes. His unfailing sympathy and compassion brought many a priest back to the full exercise of his ministry. The canon to whom I warmed most, however, was John Collins. His courageous stand for nuclear disarmament all round, his support for prisoners of conscience in South Africa and his vehement pacifism combined with friendliness and humour, drew us closely together and prepared me for later duties in Australia and the Middle East.

The four canons undertook the duties of canon-in-residence in monthly turn. During his month in residence the particular canon was in charge of the cathedral on behalf of the Dean and Chapter, and it was he who had to deal with unexpected emergencies or opportunities. He had to write the minutes of the weekly meetings of the Chapter on Saturday mornings. Even if Christmas Day fell on a Saturday the canon-in-residence had to be in the Chapter House for the weekly meeting, though the minutes for that occasion were reduced to one sentence saying that he was the only canon present and so all business was postponed until the following Saturday.

To be appointed a canon of St Paul's was one of the loveliest things that could ever happen to an Anglican priest. Morning and afternoon service were held each day with the magnificent choir on duty, and to sit in the stalls and hear the lovely singing of the psalms and the canticles and the anthem was to be lifted in heart and given a foretaste of the worship of heaven. I shall never forget the singing of the 150th Psalm which always ended the Sung Eucharist on Sunday mornings. At the daily morning service there would perhaps be only half a dozen people besides the clergy and the choir, but at evensong there might be as many as two hundred. The thing that bothered me most in the daily services was the lectionary of Bible lessons, which often seemed of little illumination or inspiration for the visitors who came to the cathedral for the afternoon service, perhaps at the end of a tour round the cathedral or sometimes for the glory of the music. The canon-in-residence always arranged for the readers of the two lessons; in most cases he would read the second lesson himself. On Easter Day 1963 I was asked if I would read the first lesson. I replied that I would be glad to do so if I could be permitted to change the set lesson, which was the account of the angel of death slaying the firstborn of Egypt. This seemed to me both untrue to my understanding of the universality of God and also completely inappropriate to Easter Day. I wanted to substitute a lesson from Isaiah 25 which contained the words, "He will swallow up death for ever, and the Lord God will wipe away tears from all faces." I was not permitted to make the desired change, and so sadly but firmly I declined to read the set lesson.

To be Archdeacon of London as well as a canon of St Paul's was an additional gift, for the archdiaconal duties were limited to the deanery of the City and to the neighbouring one of Shoreditch, the main administrative duties of the diocese being undertaken by the other archdeacons, of Hackney, Middlesex and Hampstead. The Archdeacon of London was the Bishop's representative at the cathedral end in the City, with a pastoral responsibility for the City churches.

Every Monday morning the Bishop of London had a meeting of his suffragan bishops and archdeacons at Fulham Palace, when the affairs of the diocese would be looked at, problems discussed, suggestions for vacant livings made and sometimes the need for clergy to change to a new parish if, either for the sake of the priest concerned or possibly for the parish, it seemed good that he should leave. This weekly meeting was unhurried and usually went on until all the business put before it by the bishop had been dealt with. It was an excellent training ground for any member of it who might later move to the post of a full diocesan. When I went to Perth I realised what a splendid training I had received from Robert Stopford and my colleagues, and tried to do something of the same kind for the senior clergy of Perth.

Part of the archdeacon's duty was to license the churchwardens of the parishes within his archdeaconry. Most of the City churches had more than the customary two churchwardens, and to be appointed a churchwarden was considered by many to be the first step for advancement in City representation. I tried to find out a little about the churchwardens who came to be installed, and was deeply interested to discover that among them were the chairmen of five of the leading national banks. I discussed this discovery with my closest friend among the City clergy, Norman Motley, the rector of St Michael's Cornhill, who claimed two of the five. Together we put forward the idea that these five leading bankers should be invited to a dinner with the Bishop, Norman Motley and myself, so that they could discuss how Christians in such responsible positions could rightly exercise their discipleship. As a result of this experiment, the churchwarden-bankers decided to meet for dinner every quarter. No spectacular consequences followed, but a slightly enlarged group continued to meet regularly. At the early meetings, and without doubt at the later ones as well, the clergy present did little of the talking, much to their own benefit as well as to the stimulation of lay participation.

I had been at St Paul's little more than a year when I was approached by clergy in Western Australia to enquire if I would consider an invitation to become Archbishop of Perth. This came as a disturbing surprise and my first inclination was to turn it down out of hand, feeling that I had not done anything like my duty to St Paul's. However, I thought I ought just to mention the offer to Bishop Wand, who had previously been Archbishop of Brisbane. He was a little critical of my reluctance to go further, saying that if the Church felt that I was the right person for some particular part of its work, I ought to give it very serious consideration. So I went a little further, and enquired why people in Western Australia wanted an Englishman and what they hoped for in thinking of me. The reply was both unexpected and perceptive: churchmen in Perth realised that Australia was now part of the Asian neighbourhood and wanted someone who had served the ministry in Asia to help them adjust to this new relationship. This perceptive reasoning seemed convincing and was confirmed by Bishop Stopford and Dean Matthews as well as Bishop Wand. When the invitation finally came, it was Bishop Wand who added further reasons for acceptance. With his experience of London, he said that however good a man was, and I was not all that good, he could not change the City of London, adding that in England we were busy writing history, but in Australia they had the opportunity of making history. So with some trepidation I accepted.

The West Australians asked that I should be consecrated in England, a request that I was very reluctant to fall in with, and for a month or two I tried to argue the case with them. They were adamant in saying that they wanted me to arrive as Archbishop, with authority from Canterbury, the mother see of all Anglican Churches. The Archbishop fixed St John the Baptist day, 24th June, for the consecration. This fell within my month as canon-in-residence, and for the last week of the month I carried on my cathedral duties. Seventeen bishops who were all friends and most of whom had had some hand in my past, joined in the laying on of hands. I still remember the weight of their hands upon my head, as if I were being pressed down into the very foundations of the cathedral. I had felt quietly at peace all through the service, but at the end was told that Bishop George West, who had been my diocesan in Rangoon, had collapsed with a heart attack during the service and had been taken to St Bartholomew's hospital. I hurried off to be with him and his wife, and the reception in the Chapter House took place without my presence at it until the very end. I had spent three days in quiet retreat with George West before the consecration, and owed him a great debt of gratitude for the deep and personal way in which we had tried to prepare.

Early in July my wife and I left for Perth by sea, and were glad to get a quiet time after the handing over of responsibilities and the packing of books and furniture, as well as the regret in leaving so many friends and such a lovely post.

CHAPTER 15

The Heart of a Bishop

For my consecration the Archbishop of Canterbury, Michael Ramsey, had sent me the following message:

I want to send you my joyful greetings and assurance of my prayer. There is, I believe, a specially deep joy in the pastoral work which falls to a bishop and I pray that this may be yours, bringing joy to many.

There is only one counsel which I want to give you, for your bishopric will be in places and conditions about which I am ignorant, but the counsel is this – *festina lente:* attempt less than they ask of you, and less than your own wish and inclination suggest, because 1) it is all more exacting than you realise at the time, 2) unexpected calls on time and energy turn up, on top of what is already in the diary – so that space must be left in the diary vacant for the unforeseen, 3) there is no hurry – and you give more to the people if there is more quietness somewhere in your life.

He was clearly speaking of his own experience and with an uncanny evaluation of me.

On that same day I prayed at my consecration:

O Lord God, keep me humble, make me holy, fill me with faith and love, grant me wisdom to know thy will and grace to carry it out to thy glory, through Jesus Christ my Lord.

On the evening before we left England, Walter Matthews gave

155

me a prayer which he had used for himself and which he thought would be helpful to me:

Thou hast work for me to do; O Lord, show it to me; thou hast a place for me to fill; give me grace to fill it to thy glory; thou hast given me a soul to make; make thou it for me and build me into thy spiritual temple, for Jesus' sake.

I felt that I had been shown the lines on which I should try to work.

I was installed as the sixth Bishop of Perth and the fourth Metropolitan of Western Australia in St George's Cathedral, Perth, on 12th August 1963. It was a happy coincidence that the "enthronement" should take place on 12th August, for on that day in 1829 the first stone had been laid of a new town to be called Perth, near to the entrance to the estuary of the Swan River. When I knocked at the cathedral door, asking for admission, I used a small block of wood taken from the tree under which the first Anglican service was held in 1829. The whole service, including the sermon, was televised, so many people scattered in the little towns of the one million square miles of Western Australia were able to be involved if they wished to be so.

Shortly afterwards the Australian Broadcasting Commission asked me to be interviewed at some length, probably feeling that the independent company had stolen a march on them in offering to televise the service. After the ABC interview a minister of one of the Free Churches wrote to the Western Australian daily newspaper rather critically and hurt that I should have used the word "Nonconformist." The editor, courteously, sent the letter on to me and asked if I would like to make any reply before he printed it in the newspaper. I replied that I did not think that I had used the term, and if inadvertently I had done so, it was because in England the term had a more honourable history. In any case I apologised for my possible inadvertence. A week or two later the ABC decided to repeat the interview, and many people besides myself were watching and listening with some interest to hear if I had offended. Fortunately I had not, so all was well.

The outstanding event in the sporting life of Perth was the annual horse race for the Perth Cup. The WA Race Club marked the day by a luncheon party at which the Anglican Archbishop was always asked to say grace. I realised that the spirit and atmosphere was not conducive to a lengthy pious grace. Among an unsorted box of papers I found the following text of the grace used at my first appearance:

Lord God, we pray that in our progress through life we may run a straight race, without bumping or boring, and reach the finishing post approved by Thee the Judge and Prize-Giver of all.

I found in subsequent years an interested and expectant listening on the part of the race-going guests.

A touching little incident occurred shortly after my arrival in Western Australia. I had gone to a Christmas bazaar at one of our suburban parishes. Looking around, I noticed a shabby woman with a small boy looking longingly at some of the good things displayed for sale. I pressed the equivalent of two shillings quietly into his hand. A few minutes later I was approached by the mother who said her boy had insisted on finding me again. She explained that he wanted to know my name. When I said "George Appleton," he said, "That's my name." I could not help wondering how the original Appleton came to Australia. He may even have been transported there in the early days.

In my six years in Western Australia I felt that lay people generally had not committed themselves wholeheartedly to the Christian faith and life; I think they wanted to do so, but needed assurance in a rapidly changing world when religious faith everywhere was being challenged. In every parish the laity were expected to raise the full salary of their priest, and this needed a generous level of regular giving. It also provided a means of expressing the verdict of the parish on its vicar, for if they did not agree with him on some point or felt that he was not measuring up to his pastoral task they would almost suspend their regular giving. During my time this happened in several parishes and on the whole I felt that the implied criticism was reasonable. In one or two cases the clergy concerned tried to put matters right, in other cases I had to try to get the priest in question moved to another parish.

A very interesting feature in my six years in Western Australia came in a most unexpected way. The one theatre in Perth was built on land leased from the diocese during the time of my predecessor but one, who had wisely or otherwise drawn up the lease, which included a provision that the Archbishop should have the right to examine the plays put on by the theatre authorities. Public controversy arose when those responsible planned to stage the play *The Devils of Loudon*. The theatre officials asked me to examine the text and be present at an early rehearsal. As a result I asked them to make one or two changes, which were willingly accepted.

The consequence was that in further productions I was consulted, and one result was the production of Peter Howard's *Mr Brown Comes Down the Hill*, which was a complete success and attracted full houses for several weeks. Peter Howard was perhaps the best known journalist of the time and an enthusiastic leader of Moral Rearmament. Although not a member of that body I had a great admiration for Peter and much regretted his early death.

There was a growing interest in other religions, and I was asked to give a series of talks on ABC radio to the whole of Australia on the Christian approach to other faiths. The university of Western Australia invited me on several occasions to speak at its annual extramural conference, one of the stimulating subjects given to me being "There are no heathen".

I was glad to quote a paragraph from the preface to the Old Testament in the Revised Version of the Bible published in 1884:

The Hebrew word *goyim*, "nations", which is applied to the

nations of Canaan dispossessed by the Hebrews and then also to the surrounding nations among whom the people of Israel were afterwards dispersed, acquired in later times a moral significnce which is represented in the Authorised Version by the rendering "heathen" or "Gentiles". While recognising this moral sense of the word the revisers have employed it much more sparingly than their predecessors had done.

I firmly refuse to use the word "heathen", even when it occurs in psalms or prayers, for in my contacts with people of other faiths I have found so many good things that I am quite clear that in some way God is at work among them as among us Christians.

Australian people on the whole are very forthright and not unwilling to express their reactions quite forcefully. Early one morning I was rung up on the telephone and heard a rather peremptory voice asking, "Are you the Anglican Archbishop of Perth?" On being assured that I was, my caller went on, "I'm going to shoot you." I asked good-humouredly what was the reason for this threat.

He said that on the previous day he had heard me on television expressing my opposition to a proposal that licensed brothels should be opened in Perth. I explained that my reason was the desire to avoid exploiting the women of the brothels, to which he retorted that as he was quite unattractive to women, his only hope of sex life was with prostitutes. Continuing in a friendly vein I ventured the opinion that ugly men were attractive to quite a number of women and added that I myself was not a particularly handsome chap but had a very affectionate wife, whereupon he said that he would not shoot me, but he would shoot my wife. At this point the conversation became rather more heated on both sides and we rang off simultaneously.

Early in my episcopate a leading lay member in a position of considerable responsibility, said to me that he hoped I would not appeal to the business leaders of Perth to help the Church financially. When I asked the reason for this request, he replied that the diocese had some most valuable properties in the heart of Perth and were not developing them in a responsible way which would enable the central administration of the diocese to be adequately provided for. I was able to get a former colleague in London, the Archdeacon of Hackney who managed the finances of the London diocese, to spend some weeks in Western Australia talking to the lay people and getting them to see how they could increase diocesan resources. Archdeacon Hodgins was both able and persuasive, and his visit resulted in a real break-through, and set an example of how an English diocese could help an overseas diocese from its own experience.

On the other hand, I felt that the laity were rather hard in their criticism of the clergy, who were as human and fallible as lay folk, and from time to time I had to stress to criticising parish leaders that God's forgiveness is equally available to the clergy as to the laity. On one occasion when a very angry complainant had accused one of the clergy, he claimed that the clergy ought to live to a much higher standard than the laity; when I told him that there had been argument in the Church for six hundred years or more about whether the sacraments were invalidated or not by the unworthiness of the minister, he was quite taken aback, but after reflection he felt that earlier generations had had to deal with the same problems, failures and criticisms. Yet it must be added that on the whole the clergy were a devoted lot of men, constantly travelling round very large parishes and faithfully visiting farms and homesteads many miles away from the parish centre.

Another occasion comes back in my memory, when an angry woman stirred up by something I had said about our duty to less fortunate nations said, "I have only one thing to say to you – go home, Pommy Commie." The term "Communist" was often used in Australia to decry anyone insistent on social reform.

It was shortly after my arrival in Perth that the Australian government decided to support the USA in its intervention in Vietnam. A group of Australian bishops felt that this was a mistake, and seven of us signed a letter to Mr Menzies the Prime

Minister, expressing our regrets. The letter, with the Prime Minister's reply, was published in the press throughout Australia and aroused considerable discussion. My feeling was that we could do more to arrest the spread of communism in Asia by friendly interest and generous help in Asian countries, and by so doing might help our American friends in their purpose of containing communism rather than by a token involvement in a war in which napalm and defoliation destruction were used in addition to the conventional methods. I had an inkling that the government's decision to take part in Vietnam was dictated by the desire to have American support at a time when Britain was more and more withdrawing its defence responsibilities.

We had some very lively discussions in the Synod of Bishops, and one controversial subject was the question of the remarriage in church of anyone who had been divorced. One of the provisions in the constitution of the Australian Church allowed individual bishops to exercise a right of deviation under certain circumstances. About six diocesan bishops were very concerned about remarriage, for divorce was both easy and common in Australia, and we felt that people needed the grace of God in their new marriage to avoid the failures of the first. So together we tried to work out conditions which we thought needed to be accepted if a ceremony in church was to be permitted. These included evidence that the first marriage was completely irrecoverable, that adequate provision had been made for the first family, that some responsibility for the failure had been recognised, and that remarriage in church would be accompanied by a desire and resolution to put one's life under the direction of God. In the years following this approach I think I gave permission for perhaps twenty couples to be married, and withheld permission from about the same number of people who were only anxious for a white wedding in the more dignified setting of a church rather than a registry office. Occasionally the parish priest concerned would feel unable to conduct the wedding, in which case I would take it myself; I would stress with the clergy the need of continuing pastoral care. Since I left Australia the General Synod has been considering a canon to deal with the whole question of remarriage, a draft of which my deviationist colleagues and I had started to prepare. In the back of my mind there was always the memory of Walter Matthews saying to me that, as it was the responsibility of the bishop to bind and loose, he hoped that in my case there would be occasions when I would be willing and courageous enough to exercise some loosing authority.

I had always had the hope that one day the priesthood would be open to women as well as to men. At the Lambeth Conference of 1968 the bishops expressed the view that deaconesses were truly deacons of the Church, though of course their decision was only an expression of their own conviction and in no way constitutionally binding. So on my return to Perth from Lambeth I included in the licence to deaconesses permission to assist in the administration of Holy Communion with the agreement of the vicar and the parochial church council of the parish involved. This seemingly unilateral action aroused the angry criticism of several episcopal colleagues and there was a move to express censure in the Episcopal Synod. After the critics had stated their case, the Primate, Philip Strong, asked me to reply. My reply was very short: "For over fifty years laymen have been authorised to assist in the distribution of the consecrated elements in Holy Communion, with the consent of the bishop, the parish priest and the parochial church council. Are women to be regarded as members of the laity or not?" This answer was judged to be conclusive and the Synod decided to grant permission under the same circumstances to lay members, men or women, to administer the paten or the chalice, it being agreed that it was an easier operation to distribute the host.

One thing that I was delighted to be able to do in Australia was to commend to the immigration department at Canberra applications from Anglo-Burmans to come and settle in Australia. They felt that they were not wanted any longer in Burma, and in order to found a new homeland where they could settle happily, were prepared to leave Burma with only a very limited amount of money. The Australian government was very sympathetic and there grew up a very considerable Anglo-Burmese community in Perth, who were as faithful churchpeople in Australia as they had been in Burma. Seven years after I left Perth an appeal was made to assist the very poorly paid clergy in Burma with a present of a sack of rice for Christmas 1976. I informed my Anglo-Burman friends in Perth about this appeal, and in several weeks the sum of six hundred pounds was contributed, not only valuable in itself but also challenging to old Burma friends in Britain to respond equally generously, which they did.

Ecumenical relationships in Perth were both easy and fruitful. There were representatives of the Free Churches present at my installation, and the Roman Catholic Archbishop of Perth sent a warm message of welcome and blessing; in addition representatives of the Jewish community were also present in the cathedral. The West Australian Council of Churches was an active body, though handicapped by having only one Secretary. I was its President for several years and then decided that this office ought to go round in rotation. At later meetings of this Council the question of intercommunion arose, and it was agreed that we should all take part in a concelebration, with representatives of three churches sharing the service and saying the prayer of consecration together. Unfortunately the Roman Catholic Church did not yet feel able to take part. However, considerable progress was made, for an ABC televising of friendly conversation between the RC Bishop of Bunbury and myself aroused considerable interest. Later, when that bishop was appointed RC Archbishop of Perth, representatives from the other churches were invited to his enthronement, and Anglican bishops were asked to take their place in the procession of bishops, the exact position being determined by years of consecration.

Intermarriage between Romans and Anglicans often took place, and by the rules of the Roman Church could only be solemnised in a Catholic church. I always put before the couple wanting to be married the advantages of being able to worship together as man and wife in the same church and urged both to consider prayerfully whether one should change to the church of the other.

163

This did not happen in any of the intermarriages with which I was involved, but a welcome step forward was made when I was invited to take some part in the Roman service, usually being asked to preach the sermon. The climax came when the son of the Governor was married in the Roman cathedral to a Catholic bride, where I was again invited to give a short address. Afterwards many of the Romans present expressed their gratitude for the way in which I was able to speak understandingly and humanly of the meaning of marriage and the grace of God available to the new couple to help them grow together in ever-deepening love.

Another matter in which I became deeply involved was that of the auxiliary ministry. With almost every parish priest having to minister to several widely separated congregations, Holy Communion was generally celebrated only once a month in most churches. Had there been any trained supply of auxiliary priests, this central sacrament could have been a weekly participation, a vital opportunity for a Church that claimed to be sacramental. I had realised what a great pastoral contribution could be made in this way, from my experience in Burma and my knowledge of the number of villages in India in which a single-handed priest had to try to supply the sacramental means of grace. So following the inspiration of the Southwark training course we instituted a similar plan for the diocese of Perth. We were fortunate in having a priest with considerable theological understanding and pastoral care, and under his leadership a number of men enrolled for one evening's seminar a week, with occasional weekends together. The plan had only started to mature when I left Perth; it was discontinued by my successor, who felt that the supply of candidates for the formal ministry was sufficient for the diocese. I remember one candidate for the supplementary ministry who seemed to understand its purpose even more deeply than I did myself, for he recognised that the main task was not to fill in for the whole-time clergy or relieve them during holidays or sickness, but to exercise a priestly responsibility within his own profession in a relevant and quiet way. One great consolation came to me when my son Timothy felt a call to join the Southwark course, having the same understanding of his ministry as my promising candidate in Perth.

Another involvement in contemporary issues came through the protracted suffering of a sister of the Church who had undergone two operations for cancer. I visited her in hospital every day during a period of six months, whenever I was in Perth and not away on outside visits or duties. We were able to talk very deeply about the mystery of suffering, and one day when the ultimate issue seemed certain, the sister asked me, "Father, would it be wrong if I gradually decreased my intake of food and drink, so that I would no longer be a burden to others as well as to myself?" We quoted to one another St Paul's words to his friends at Philippi that on his own part he would much prefer to depart and be with Christ. I expressed my understanding of her position and motive, but said that we had better be guided by the advice of the medical staff. The Matron, herself a good Christian woman, said that if the course hinted at was put into practice, contemporary medical opinion would prescribe forcible feeding. As a result we went on trying to understand the problem of suffering, in the assurance that God's loving grace would be sufficient for both the pain of body and the travail of mind and spirit. More than ten years later this question has become a more pressing one, though its final solution has not yet appeared. Clearly it could vary in individual instances.

In July 1968 at the Lambeth Conference I was asked to be the convenor of a section or group dealing with the relationship of Christianity to other faiths. We did not get very far in our section, for some of the bishops were firmly opposed to any positive relationship for fear that our own devotion to Jesus Christ and his uniqueness should be endangered. The report of this section was scarcely mentioned in the first draft of the main section on "The Renewal of the Church in Faith", and I felt impelled to get up in a full session of the conference to urge the point that others besides Christians were involved in understanding the religious experience and faith and could supply some light on the vital questions under discussion. In the end the conference passed three relevant resolutions:

> The Conference invites the Archbishop of Canterbury on its behalf to consult with the Pope and the Ecumenical Patriarch and the Praesidium of the World Council of Churches on the possibility of approaching leaders of the other world religions with a view to convening a conference at which in concert they would speak in the interests of humanity on behalf of world peace.

> It is the conviction of the Conference that, in their obedience to Christ's mission and command and in their obligation towards the contemporary world, the Christian Churches must endeavour such positive relationship to the different religions of men, and to the doubts and denial of faith as will
>> set forward the common unity of mankind and a common participation in its present history;
>> encourage Christians to increasing co-operation with men of other faiths in the fields of economic, social and moral action;
>> call Christians not only to study other faiths in their own seriousness but also to study unbelief in its reality.

> The Conference recommends a renewed and vigorous implementation of the task of inter-religious dialogue already set in hand in the study centres organised by the World Council of Churches and other bodies, and urges increased Anglican support both in the seconding of personnel and in the provision of money. It also commends similar assistance for dialogue with Marxists and those who profess no religious faith.

Looking back on my years in Western Australia I realise the debt I owe to a number of people. Foremost among these was Brian Macdonald, the Archdeacon of Perth and Commissary

during the interregnum between the resignation of my predecessor and my arrival. He was so wise spiritually and so humble
that I still cannot understand why the diocese and the province
did not choose him as Archbishop. I fancy that he had a big voice
in my nomination, for he valued so highly the books of prayers
that I had collected or written, was fully sympathetic to my vision
of the Church in the world, and so loyal in trying to ensure that
the decisions I had to make should be both accepted and fruitful.
We spent regular hours together sharing with one another our
deepest thoughts, and crystallised what was needed for the
renewal of the life of the Church. The diocese had agreed that
when I came there should be an assistant bishop and as far as
they or I were concerned, there was only one candidate, namely
Brian Macdonald. He had come out to Australia as a boy settler,
he knew the conditions in other parts of the continent and the
people who could give insight and advice, and he had both the
affection and courage to raise with me questions that he felt
needed to be answered before any course of action was undertaken.

A friend whose generous support enabled me to carry out the
task more effectively was Tom Wardle, the head of a chain of
supermarkets numbering over a hundred, mainly in Western
Australia but also in other parts as well. He was generous enough
and rash enough to ask me in my early days in what way a gift
of money from him could forward the work. The answer came
immediately – to enable me to have a whole-time chaplain.
Thereupon "Tom the Cheap Grocer" as he was popularly known,
promised the complete support of a chaplain, and I was able to
invite Jeremy Harold, who had been trained as chaplain to Bishop
Stopford of London. Later, when Archbishop Ramsey visited
Australia, Tom made available his private plane to fly him to
certain centres in Western Australia and thus enabled him to visit
a greater part of the Church. Later still he provided annual grants
for the support of three chaplains to the University of Western
Australia, a Roman Catholic, an Anglican and a Free Church
minister. His final gift was to found an annual lecture in the

University on some subject of biblical and theological interest. Tom was a simple, straightforward, naturally Christian person, a man of few words and even fewer letters, whose generosity and integrity resulted in his being elected as Lord Mayor of Perth, and in due time being given a knighthood.

A third person to whom I owe much gratitude is Catharine King, who was in charge of the women's section of radio in Western Australia. She had a daily programme for women which was eagerly listened to by almost as many men. I took part in many of her programmes in which her technique was to put me on some sensitive spot of her own choosing and follow this up with question after question, often drawing out from me thoughts and crystallised convictions of which I had not been conscious before her searching and kindly cross-examination.

A further intimate friend was Irwin Crowe, an artist, who had little church affiliation but deep spiritual searching to get to the heart of things and to express them through his art of painting and copper-and-enamel craft. He designed the chapel in Archbishop's House in Perth, which my wife and I had been able to retrieve when a long lease ran out. I still have in my small study a cross which he made in varying shades of flaming red, which speaks to me every time I look at it of sacrifice, love and spiritual fire.

There are many others whom I remember with warm gratitude, a whole crowd of trusting churchpeople who wanted a message from God to enlighten their understanding and to supply the morale needed for a rapidly changing world.

One of the most moving incidents in my time in Western Australia took place on the night before I presided at the consecration of Howell Witt as Bishop of North Western Australia. Late that night he came to my house and put to me this question: "If you were asked to say just one thing, and one thing only, to a priest about to be consecrated as a bishop, what would you say?" Somehow the answer came immediately, without any exercise of thought: "I would put to him the question which Jesus put to James and John in their ambition for chief place in the

Kingdom – 'Can you drink the cup that I have to drink?' " He asked me to explain further, and I tried to explain something of the cost of being a bishop, how often one was under pointed criticism but was prevented from reply or explanation by the pastoral confidentiality involved in a situation; that a bishop came to know of the failures, personal and pastoral, in the lives of his clergy; that he bore on his heart the burden of the spiritual poverty of his people, as well as the knowledge of his own weaknesses and mistakes. All this involved a bitter cup.

Over four years later Bishop Howell Witt came to see me late on the night before I left Perth, after all the farewells, formal and individual. He asked me if I remembered the question he had put to me four years earlier, and when I said that I should never forget that question, he added, "I just want to tell you that what you told me has been borne out in experience. Thank you once again."

CHAPTER 16

City of Peace?

I was able to attend only one Lambeth Conference, the one in 1968. It was during that conference that the Archbishop in Jerusalem, Campbell MacInnes, announced his resignation. Knowing nothing of this intended resignation, my wife and I arranged to visit Jerusalem on our journey to Lambeth. I naturally called on Campbell, whom I had known quite intimately when I was on the staff of Edinburgh House and he was a suffragan bishop in a diocese close to London.

Shortly after Lambeth, I wrote to Archbishop Michael Ramsey to commend Canon Kenneth Cragg to fill this important vacancy. He had spent a number of years in Beirut and had written a remarkable book, entitled *The Call of the Minaret*, which studied sympathetically and deeply the spirituality of Islam, and which had been a key book in my own approach to people of other faiths. I heard nothing from Archbishop Michael for nearly three months, when I received a letter written in his own hand, thanking me for the interesting suggestion I had made and saying that he now made what he said was a more interesting suggestion, namely that I should go to Jerusalem. I still felt that my suggestion of Kenneth Cragg, who had been Warden of St Augustine's College, Canterbury, and had been very sad that it was no longer to be a missionary college, should be more positively considered. So I wrote to Max Warren, who by this time was recognised as an outstanding missionary statesman, as well as a warm personal friend, asking him to go into the whole question and if he felt Kenneth was the right man for the Jerusalem archbishopric, I would decline it. Max went into the matter more deeply than I had even hoped, and after several weeks wrote to say that his advice was that I should succeed Campbell McInnes, and that I should make provision for Kenneth to become assistant bishop within a year. The result was that I obediently accepted Archbishop Michael's plan, for he had been in ready consultation with Max, who made the point that Kenneth would be back in the Middle East and free to continue his invaluable relationship with Muslims.

I have explained this background at some length, for it was a creative and decisive moment for both Kenneth and myself, with the promise of a balanced colleagueship, both of its members wanting it to be an agreed devotion to the will of God as far as we could discover it, and having a deepening desire for that joint venture to be inspired and directed by the divine wisdom and grace.

There was not much time for spiritual preparation, but it soon became clear that some words of St Paul in his second letter to the Christians of Corinth supplied the inspiration:

> God gave us the ministry of reconciliation . . . entrusting
> to us the message of reconciliation. So we are ambassadors
> for Christ, God making his appeal through us. (5:18-20)

So, commissioned and blessed by the Archbishop of Canterbury, in the presence of a large congregation of lovers of Jerusalem and the Middle East, my wife and I flew out to Tel Aviv, where a group of Jerusalem clergy and Israeli officials welcomed us at the airport, their speeches and my reply being recorded by Israel radio.

I learned later that the Arab clergy of the diocese of Jerusalem and Jordan, numbering less than twenty in all, had held a meeting to discuss whether they should take any part in the formal receptions to me. They had been pressing for the appointment of an Arab successor to Archbishop MacInnes, their hope being that Bishop Cubaing, the Arab bishop of the Jordan diocese, might be chosen. It was under Bishop Cubaing's persuasion that they agreed to join in the welcome and to take

171

the oath of obedience to their new diocesan.

A further complication was in the wording of the Archbishop of Canterbury's licence which I thought might cause offence. I had been uneasy about this wording when it was read out at the service of authorisation at Lambeth. Fortunately very few at the Jerusalem ceremony understood its legal wording, but I became even more disquieted and one of the Jerusalem canons confirmed my suspicions, though he himself was a strong supporter of the Arabs. So the licence was withdrawn, corrected and re-issued by the ecclesiastical authorities in London. The explanation was that the lawyers had merely copied the wording that had been used at the installation of Archbishop MacInnes, regardless of the constitutional changes that had taken place in the interval.

I inherited one legacy from my predecessor for which I was deeply grateful. This was in the form of his adviser on Jewish and Israeli affairs, the Reverend Peter Schneider, born a Jew, adopted by a Christian society as an orphan and baptised by them as a Christian. Peter was invaluable to my predecessor and loyal to us both. Confronted by an outstanding Jewish scholar with the angry question, "Is this new archbishop of yours on our side or on that of the Palestinians?" Peter, with perceptiveness, retorted, "He is on both sides!" When some time later Peter was appointed a canon of St George's Cathedral and the promises relative to that appointment were in Hebrew, there was an angry protest from Amman that Hebrew had never been used before in the cathedral, which showed a profound ignorance of the history of the Jerusalem bishopric.

It was through Peter that I came to know, trust and love Teddy Kollek, the Mayor of Jerusalem. He had been present at my installation and had been moved by my plea for understanding and reconciliation. The 1967 war had resulted in many families becoming separated by the river Jordan frontier. I soon became aware of this family separation and began to work for its amelioration. I referred appeals for family reunions to Teddy, who said that he would help wherever humanly possible, provided I would leave him free to make his own enquiries as to the truthfulness of each application for permission to return to Jerusalem. With his co-operation I was also allowed to visit any Israeli prisons in which political prisoners were held, and even to take them small luxuries from their families and myself.

Teddy Kollek, as mayor and administrator for the reunited city, cared for the welfare of all its members, including the 80,000 Arabs in East Jerusalem, who when the time came for the periodical election of the mayor, voted solidly for him. Teddy called together regularly meetings of a Jerusalem Advisory Committee, which he pressed me to join. I felt unable to accept membership, but asked if I might be accepted as a consultant, who would try to work for reconciliation and peace. This was accepted, and I found it of great help in my own pastoral responsibilities.

The plan for an assistant bishop developed successfully, and within six months of my arrival Kenneth Cragg was consecrated, to our great joy. It was agreed that he should live in Cairo, so as to be in touch with Arab and Muslim scholars there, who were of higher standing than those in Jerusalem. I, as a matter of course, took the small Anglican community into my confidence. They quite unexpectedly had some misgivings, and insisted that I, like my predecessor, should be regarded as the acting bishop in the suspended diocese of Egypt, and Kenneth should be my representative. The reason behind this, which I only discovered later, was their hope for an Egyptian bishop. They had in mind a very promising young priest in old Cairo, whom they hoped to send to Britain for wider training. They saw that because of my age I was likely to stay only a few years, whereas Kenneth was a good ten years younger than me and could stay for ten years after I had retired. So all was agreed, if for different reasons. During his time in Cairo, Kenneth was to be closely involved in planning the new cathedral. For myself it was an intriguing situation to be Archbishop in Jerusalem and acting Bishop in Egypt, and also an imperative to be a peacemaker.

In Jerusalem there was no officially constituted ecumenical body. There was considerable rivalry between the three Patriarchs – Orthodox, Armenian and Latin – as to their rights in the Church

173

of the Holy Sepulchre (which some of us preferred to speak of as the Church of the Resurrection). All three Patriarchs graciously came to my installation, at which service they listened carefully to my address. Any ecumenical relationship had to be developed through friendly contacts, and it soon dawned on me that part of my vocation should be to visit, get to know and then ask guidance from those three seniors.

A practice had grown up over the years in which the head of each Church paid a formal visit to the heads of all the other Churches during the three days following the festivals of Christmas and Easter. The routine was the same. The visitor and his accompanying dignitaries would be received into the large audience chamber, and introduced to the Patriarch or host sitting in his seat of authority. He would make a short speech of welcome, and small glasses of brandy and appropriate delicacies would be served. The visitor would raise any contemporary questions of interest; small cups of Turkish coffee would be brought in, which was understood by hosts and visitors alike as a polite indication that the hospitality was now ending. Four, or sometimes five, such visits were made in a morning, involving four or five small but potent glasses of brandy, produced in Latrun monastery, not far from Tel Aviv.

The Anglican Archbishop in Jerusalem had a pastoral responsibility for Anglicans in twenty-two different countries, mainly in the Gulf and in North Africa, including the Sudan and Ethiopia. It was an almost impossible task in a time of cold war always in danger of becoming inflamed to something worse. Yet it offered commensurate opportunities for peacemaking, even if Arab extremists could not imagine that anyone who had his headquarters in Jerusalem could possibly be an open-minded ambassador of peace. The British Foreign Office helpfully issued me with three different passports to use in different situations. That certainly eased matters for me, and satisfied national pride, but it also involved tactical foresight and skill in presenting the right passport at each inspection and keeping the other two tactfully hidden.

I had not been settled long in Jerusalem when I was visited by two people who were to become friends and allies. The first was an Arab journalist who had just returned from a tour of America and Europe. He told me that in quite a number of places he had been urged to call on me. His name was Jamil Hamad and his office, which was a meeting place for foreign correspondents, was only a few hundred yards away from St George's Cathedral. He was a quiet worker for peace, and was skilled in briefing me about the quickly changing political situation. In return I was able to help him with the education of his three sons, and occasionally with travelling expenses. Time and time again his assessments were perceptive and accurate.

Jamil had his critics and detractors. On one occasion he was falsely accused of a political murder. As soon as I heard about this, I went to the prison where he was being held and asked if I might visit him. The governor of the prison asked somewhat sharply what right had I to intervene and when I replied that I knew the prisoner well, and that the alleged crime was completely contrary to his peaceable nature, I was allowed to see and comfort my friend without anyone being present to overhear our conversation. That incident took place just before Easter, and my official visitor on Easter Monday was the minister in charge of police and prisons. After the usual friendly exchanges I asked him what he was planning to do with my friend Hamad. He replied, "What would you do if you were in my place?" My reply was that I would release him first thing next morning. He then asked if I was prepared to stand surety for him, to which I replied without hesitation that I would gladly do so. The outcome was that the next morning Jamil smilingly turned up at Bishop's House. The official announcement was that the Anglican Archbishop had stood surety for him. Nothing further was heard of the charges made against him.

The second unexpected visit happened in this way. One morning my excellent secretary Jean Waddell came into my study to say that a certain gentleman would be grateful if he could see me. She said that he had given his name as Boegner and that he was a son of Pastor Boegner, the head of the French Reformed Church. This was a thrill for me, for I had heard the father speak at a conference of the World Council of Churches, of which he was a President. So I met the son, Etienne, for the first time. He said he had come to ask for my interest in making a garden of prayer on the Mount of Olives, in memory of his father and of Pope Paul VI who had been his dear friend.

Etienne Boegner was a welcome visitor at the great convent of St Etienne (St Stephen), where the Dominican Fathers lived, with their well-known Ecole Biblique and library and their links with their French homeland. In a very short time I became as welcome as Etienne and was often invited to lunch and to small meetings of biblical and archaeological scholars. The great church was halfway between St George's and the Damascus Gate, the main entry into the Old City.

The piece of land on which Etienne had his eye was a garden owned by the Sisters of Sion, and which was used as a picnic centre for the pupils of a girls' school which they had formerly administered. It had in it some magnificent olive trees said to be centuries old. Etienne formed a trust of which he asked me to be the president. Negotiations with the Sisters and with their central community in Rome took several years to complete. It was finally decided to lease it to the trust at a peppercorn rent. Etienne Boegner set aside a generous sum to lay out the garden and holding walls and organise drainage. From its main platform there was the most glorious view of the walled city, with the two mosques, the Dome of the Rock with its golden cupola and the Al-Aksa with a silver one, also the Church of the Resurrection, and in the far distance the tower of St George's Cathedral.

The Sisters of Sion had their convent in the Via Dolorosa, with its entrance almost under the Ecce Homo arch. They had been founded to make liaison with Judaism, and were fortunate in having some great and ancient water tanks which visitors thronged to see, and a great platform which had clearly been the waiting place for the Roman garrison. Some archaeologists have

176

claimed it to be the Praetorium where Jesus was held, scourged and mocked as his captors waited for dawn.

The Sisters were very shrewd in their planning. They arranged weekly courses for Arabs who wanted to learn Hebrew and for Israelis who wanted to learn Arabic. They assembled the same day of the week, in different halls, for their language study, but there was only one refreshment centre at one time and so Arabs and Israelis met and got to know something of each other.

I have already said that twenty-two different countries were in my pastoral care, so quite half my time was spent outside Jerusalem and the Holy Land. Before going on any particular tour I made a practice of calling on a leading member of the Israeli cabinet and asking him what I might say about the hope of peace, and on my return reporting to the same minister what was being said in the countries visited. I can't say that there was any spectacular success, but at least one person was trying to bridge the gap.

One incident remains in my memory. One day just before the annual Jewish festival there was a disastrous fire in the Al-Aksa mosque. Immediately suspicions were aroused and rumours circulated that Israelis had been responsible, and in any case had failed to protect the holy place. Accusations and fears brought tensions to the whole city. On the following Sunday, as part of the festival celebrations, a great concert was given in the largest hall available. The programme was a rendering of the Bethlehem Cantata, the words written by a Spanish poet, the music composed by the great cellist Pablo Casals, who himself conducted part of the oratorio and played a small part in the music, although he was ninety-three years old and clearly frail. The choruses were sung in English by joint choirs from the Israeli Kibbutzim. At the end there was tremendous applause and Pablo Casals, greatly moved, stood up before the big audience, opened his arms wide and said, "I love you all! I love you all!" I couldn't help thinking that there could not have been a more healing touch after such a week of tension, anxiety, and fear.

Ultimately it was discovered that the fire had been started by a mentally sick Australian. I arranged for my chaplain Maurice Coombs, himself an Australian, to go to the prison and visit him. He reported back that the arsonist was sitting cross-legged on his bed, not only without any remorse, but nonchalantly pleased with himself.

I was often in Amman, visiting Bishop's Boys School which was founded by one of my predecessors and always reckoned to be the personal affair and responsibility of the current diocesan, and supported from his funds. To get into Jordan one had to cross the Allenby bridge. On one occasion as I set out from Jerusalem someone called out, "Bring some cholera vaccine back with you!" On arrival I enquired from the head man how I might procure some vaccine, and was told that it could only be obtained from the government factory. Fortunately the headmaster, David Tonkin, a New Zealander, was a great friend of the Jordanian official in charge of the factory. On the day before I was due to return to Jerusalem a message came saying that if I was at the factory by six o'clock the next morning a supply would be waiting for me. I was there on time, and the boot of my car was filled with cardboard boxes full of stone-cold injections sufficient for several thousand patients. I anticipated some trouble from the Israeli officers on duty. I was well known to the officer-in-charge, who called out, "Nothing to declare as usual, I suppose, Archbishop." I informed him to the contrary, and on inspecting the boot he was sternly critical, saying that the vaccine would have been damaged in the heat of the morning sun, and in all probability it would have been poisoned by the Jordanians. He ordered it to be confiscated and instructed me to find refrigeration for it in the local hospital. I did as ordered and continued on my way somewhat unhappily. Five days later I got a message from the authorities saying that the vaccine was clean and had not deteriorated on the journey from Amman; I could have as much of it as I wanted for my friends in the West Bank.

There was an interesting development a fortnight later. The kind official at the Amman factory suddenly developed a tumour on the brain. Application was made to the authorities for him to be admitted to the finest hospital in Israel, the famous Hadasah Hospital. The application was quickly granted and the patient was brought by ambulance from Amman, but a few days later he died, much to my sadness. Reflection however made me feel that if this reciprocal kindness could occur at a national level the hopes for peace would be quickly realised.

In my look-back in memory I recall another memorable experience. Quite near St George's was the eye hospital founded and funded by the British Knights of St John. When Jerusalem was under Jordan until 1967, King Hussein was a great supporter of it and so were several other Arab rulers. When I first visited the hospital, I was taken to see every ward and facility. The thing that impressed me most was the room with the eye-bank, with its small store of donated eyes waiting to be transplanted. Near it was a photograph of King Hussein with an official letter signed by him, saying, "In the event of my death I bequeath my eyes to this hospital in the hope that they will enable sight to be restored to someone who has lost it.'

As I write, memory after memory comes back. Before I end this chapter I must not forget one more name that I remember with affection and gratitude, that of Archbishop Laghi, who was the Apostolic Delegate during nearly all my five years in Jerusalem. Almost weekly when not on tour I would visit him and together we would confer on what steps might be taken towards peace. When he transferred to Buenos Aires, and after that to become the Papal Nuncio in Washington, the warm friendship continued. Even while drafting this chapter I received an affectionate letter which stressed his hope that we might meet again before too long.

A verse from the Psalms expressed my feelings, and I am sure those of many other pilgrims to the City of Peace.

If I forget thee, O Jerusalem, let my right hand forget her cunning. Let my tongue cleave to the roof of my mouth, if I set not Jerusalem above my chiefest joy. (137:5-6)

CHAPTER 17

Other Faith

I count myself a very fortunate person in being able to meet so many people of different faith to my own, and being entrusted with their friendship. The result of this mutual relationship has been that we could often talk together at a deep level of our own spiritual search and experience, about the founders of our respective religions, abour our ideals of the good life, the saints of our own traditions, and how we could begin to work together for human unity and happiness.

At St Augustine's Missionary College, where I received training in spiritual life and missionary vocation, we were not taught much about other religions, and what we were taught aimed more at being able to refute their tenets and to convert them to Christianity. My first close contact with people of other faith was in my curacy at Stepney where 40 per cent of the people in the parish were Jews, many shops were owned by Jews, many patients in the local Poor Law hospital were Jews and often needed comforting as they faced serious operations or were very frightened at the possibility or probability of death. I have mentioned that one of the things that impressed me most was the friendship of my rector with the local rabbi and their respect for each other's convictions and ministries. It was not till I arrived in Burma, and saw how Buddhism had impregnated the national life, that the question of the relationship between their faith and mine became an urgent one. The life and character of Gautama, the Buddha, the Enlightened One, had been the start of a deeper study forbidding any theory of falsity. I recognised a difficulty in the fact that many Buddhists did not believe in a personal God.

The next step was to think of Christianity as the fulfilment of other faiths, but in the light of developing experience I began to feel that this was a claim of Christian superiority. My own faith in God did not waver, nor my discipleship to Jesus and his revelation of the God of love and righteousness. I remember Mrs Rhys Davids giving the title of one of her scholarly books as *The Gospel of the Buddha*. So I began to ponder in my mind the essential message or good news to mankind of each of the many religious traditions.

I naturally began to study more closely the contacts of Jesus with people who were not Jews by birth. There was the centurion, anxious about the serious illness of his son (or servant), who must have learnt something of Jesus' compassion and healing gifts, and then send messengers to him, saying, "I am not worthy that you should come under my roof. Say the word of healing only and my son will be healed." His message has become one of the gems of Christian devotion, with the appreciative comment of Jesus, "I have not found such great faith, not even in Israel."

I also remember our Lord's experience, when he had retired northward to Sidon to escape the threat to his life from King Herod. On that occasion a Syrian mother, grieved about her epileptic daughter and hearing that Jesus was in the neighbourhood, determined to appeal for his help. Jesus, perhaps to test her concern and pertinacity, said, "It is not right to take the children's food and to give it to the dogs" (barking hopefully under the table). He must have used a term which applied to the household dogs rather than to the pariah dogs roaming the streets. With her quick mother wit she replied, "Yes, Lord, but the dogs eat the crumbs which fall from their master's table." At every Christian Eucharist she is remembered when we say in one of the prayers, "We are not worthy to gather up the crumbs under thy table."

There was a second Roman centurion with whom Jesus only came in touch in the last hours of his life, in the six hours on the cross. He was in charge of the execution squad, and so had plenty of time to observe the bearing of the Jew crucified by Roman authority at the insistence of some of the Jewish leaders, and

181

hanging between two notorious thieves (or possibly rebels). All four Gospels make mention of this centurion, reported through the mind of each evangelist and expressed in the light of his own developed devotion, or perhaps implied through each writer's knowledge of the duties of a Roman officer in charge of frequent executions. Mark and Matthew record his comment as, "Truly this was the Son of God." His exact words might have been, "Truly this man was a son of the gods." Luke has "Certainly this was a righteous man," implying that he was innocent of the charges brought against him. John alone reports our Lord's words, "I thirst!", uttered shortly before his death, and goes on to say that a sponge was dipped in the sour wine that the soldiers had by them to slake their thirst during a long and hot spell of duty. It could well have been the order of the centurion to attach the sponge to a spear and lift it to the lips of the suffering Christ. We who are Christ's disciples today can be grateful to Longinus, as well as to Simon from Cyrene, an ancient Greek and Roman city of North Africa. Nor should we forget that John was standing by the cross throughout the six hours, and so would have been aware of the happenings and conversations there.

An earlier passage in the fourth Gospel contains an insight into the relation of Jesus to his mission to the world which is often not perceived and emphasised. After the resuscitation of Lazarus, there was a surge of faith in Jesus. This was reported to the religious leaders in Jerusalem, and the chief priests and Pharisees called a meeting of "the council" to consider what should be done and to avoid a dangerous confrontation with the Romans. One of them, Caiaphas, who was high priest that year, said to them, "You know nothing at all; you do not understand that it is expedient that one man should die for the people, and that the whole nation should not perish." John adds:

> He did not say this of his own accord, but being high priest that year he prophesied that Jesus should die for the nation, and not for the nation only, but to gather into one the children of God who are scattered abroad. (11:51-2)

It looks as if John may have had an idea that the high priests could receive inspiration from God, to which he adds his own perception that the task accepted by Jesus was to be the Gatherer of all the people of God, and the facets of truth which they have perceived.

The writer of the Letter to the Ephesians seems to share this perception:

> God has made known to us the mystery of his will according to his purpose which he set forth in Christ as a plan for the fulness of time, to unite all things in him, things in heaven and things on earth. (1:9-10)

He makes this mystery universal and explicit a little later:

> When you read this *(epistle)* you can perceive my insight into the mystery of Christ, which was not made known to the sons *(children)* of men in other generations as it has now been revealed to his holy apostles and prophets by the Spirit; that is, how the Gentiles are fellow heirs, members of the same body and partakers of the promise in Christ Jesus through the gospel. (3:4-6)

In Paul's letter to Timothy, "my true child in the faith," he carries on the theme: "God our Saviour desires all men to be saved and to come to the knowledge of the truth" (2:3-4).

The meaning of the salvation which God desires has nowhere been more clearly expressed than by the late Professor Geoffrey Lampe of Cambridge: "Salvation is the experienced reality of God's saving presence." If in our Christian theology we believe that God is the Creator of all, and if at the same time we believe that He has shown his nature, love and will in Jesus Christ, we must surely believe that He loves all, forgives all, and is active among all, beginning his saving work at the point at which they now are, working within that human nature until it becomes transfused and transformed into the divine nature, as set out in

183

the gem of spirituality in the second epistle attributed to Peter: "He has granted to us his precious and very great promises, that through these you may escape from the corruption that is in the world, and become partakers of the divine nature" (2 Pet. 1:4).

The vital thing is that we should accept that precious and great promise, and progressively realise that the nearer we get to God, the more conscious we become of the gap between his holiness and ours. In all our discussions with Jews, we should never forget that Jesus was born a Jew, lived as a Jew, and died a Jew.

For many centuries Christians have been guilty of anti-Semitic activities, acquiescing in or even initiating persecution of Jews. One has only to read the fulminations against Jews of St John Chrysostom (347-407), Bishop of Constantinople – whose name means "the golden-mouthed one" – to be shocked to the heart about the un-Christlike attitude which continued in the Christian Church to the nineteenth century, and was considered by many Jewish historians and writers to have been a factor making possible the holocaust of the Hitler Nazi regime. I have been a keen member of the Council of Christians and Jews (CCJ) since its foundation – it recently celebrated its fiftieth anniversary. Its patron is Her Majesty the Queen, and its joint Presidents are the Archbishop of Canterbury, the Cardinal Archbishop of Westminster, the Chief Rabbi, the Moderator of the Church of Scotland and the Moderator of the Free Church Federal Council. This guard of honour and its many members are united in a common effort to fight the evils of prejudice, intolerance and discrimination between people of different religions, races and colours, and to work for the betterment of human relations, based on mutual respect, understanding, and goodwill. To work for harmony with such splendid motives helps to redeem the past, and to bring hope for the future. (I was humbled and grateful by the award, shortly after my retirement from Jerusalem, of the Buber-Rosezweig Medal, incidentally the biggest medal I have ever seen, and one which could have well figured in Saki's famous story of the little girl who insisted on wearing her medals which clashed together when she was pursued by a wild animal, with the result that all that was left of her was the string of blood-stained medals.)

I cannot end this chapter without a mention of the Centre for Higher Biblical and Theological Studies, founded by Pope Paul VI to commemorate his visit to Jerusalem and the Holy Land. A site of many acres was provided by His Holiness at Tantur, halfway between Jerusalem and Bethlehem, together with a gift of a million pounds to lay out beautiful gardens and provide a chapel, lecture rooms, a fine assembly hall which could accommodate an audience of four hundred, as well as a library and comfortable quarters for visiting scholars from all the Christian Churches. They are expected to carry on their own research studies, but to share them with one another in ecumenical discussion and fellowship. I arrived in Jerusalem just as the Centre was ready to begin its activities, and was able to be present at the dedication. After my retirement I was invited to spend four months as a visiting student. The Governing Council was eager and determined to be generously ecumenical in its staff and invitations, alternating in the appointment of a director president. Very soon after its inauguration scholars from Judaism and Islam were invited, and public meetings were arranged to further understanding between Jews, Muslims and Christians and to work for peace in the city so dear to their own adherents. A great future lies ahead for this splendid institution, and also for the religious bodies who send delegates to take part in its creative vision and hopes.

CHAPTER 18

Seeking the Self

The longest journey
Is the journey inwards,
Of him who has chosen his destiny,
Who has started upon his quest
For the source of his being.

Dag Hammarskjöld, *Markings*

To be present at a death-bed, to see a corpse cold and lifeless, or to be present at a funeral whether by burial or by cremation, raises the question in one's mind as to what is the essence of personality. To have lived in close relationship and friendship with Buddhists is to have that question pressed on one more deeply and challengingly. One will have learnt that Buddhists recognise five constituents of being – form or matter or body, sensation or feeling, perception, mental activity, and consciousness. When these five aggregates are in combination there is life, when they disintegrate death takes place. In a discourse known as "The Marks of Non-Self" the Buddha taught:

> Body, monks, is without self: feeling, perception, mental elements and consciousness . . . whatever body there is, internal or external, coarse or fine, base or lofty, far or near, past, present or future, all that body is not mine, I am not that, that is not the self.

So declared E.J. Thomas in *The Quest of Enlightenment*, published in 1950, when I was still wrestling with the basic question. Similarly feeling, perception, mental activity, and consciousness are not the self. The Buddhist deduction from this statement from their Great Teacher is that there is no self. In a book which I wrote in 1961 I asked myself and my Buddhist friends if this was the only possible deduction. Might not Gautama the Buddha have been saying that the self is something other, something that owns, uses and directs these aggregates? Might not the Buddha in the sixth century BC have been saying something to many people in the twentieth century AD who tend to identify the body with the real person, and who at death-beds and funerals think that the end of the body is the end of being, instead of thinking of the funeral as the disposal of the outworn physical clothing, no longer the willing and obedient partner of the inner spirit or self. Today, having to live with a body that is growing tired and old and slow, the conviction has crystallised in me that the body is not the self.

I came also to see that in the teaching of the Buddha there is certainly a "self" which needs to be recognised and repudiated, an ever-changing, superficial, grasping being, the stream of feelings, thoughts, and desires, which insists on its own absolute individuality and independence. Often this self is spoken of in modern terms as the ego. This is spoken of by St Paul as the old self which has to be crucified if the new and permanent self is to live. Paul felt the power of this old self very strongly in himself. He even said "I die daily", implying that every day of his life he had to repudiate this selfish centre. Only by this self-denying could the true self take over and rule his life.

Some Buddhist friends have put this in another way – the process of becoming has to merge into being. Until it does so, one does not arrive at the further shore, and reach the bliss of perfection. There is, moreover, a sense in which the Buddha speaks more positively of the self as good and dear. In a conversation with the King of Kosala he agrees with the king's remarks to the effect that evil conduct in thought, word and deed is treating the self as a foe, and good conduct as a dear friend:

Since aye so dear the self to others is,
Let the self-lover harm no other man.

This comes very close to the second great commandment of
Judaism and Christianity, "Thou shalt love thy neighbour as
thyself," asserting that the true love of self is the measure by which
we should love others.

I make this long introduction to show to myself that my contact
with Buddhists and my reverent respect for the Buddha have been
a positive and helpful factor in a long ministry.

The search to understand one's self has been greatly stimulated
in the last hundred years by the great pioneers of psychology,
Freud, Jung and Adler. It was the second of these that thrilled me
most, particularly in his experiences and interpretation of dreams,
for from my boyhood I have been fascinated and puzzled by
frequent dreams. I have recounted in chapter 1 of this book a
recurring nightmare involving a walnut tree falling on me. I was
a boy of eight at the time. Looking back, I now realise that every
time I was afraid of some situation that dream would recur and
warn me of the fear within myself.

Another dream from later years was of being in the pulpit and
preaching what I knew to be rubbish, while the congregation
listened as if I were preaching pure truth and gospel. The result
was that I had to force myself to go up the steps of the pulpit and
preach what I had carefully prepared. That dream too recurred
quite often, until one Sunday a voice spoke to me in it, saying,
"You know they are right and you are wrong." Since that dream
happened, it has not recurred, much to my relief, for I have been
invited to preach in many churches, as well as having to preach
in the course of my pastoral responsibilities.

In more recent years a further recurring dream has puzzled me.
I am in our car, with my wife, driving to St Paul's Cathedral to
preach on a Sunday afternoon. We come in sight of the cathedral,
but cannot find the way to reach it. There is not a soul in the
streets from whom to enquire the way. We go round and round,

hoping to find an exit to St Paul's, until we realise that in any case we shall be too late for the sermon time. The only comfort in the dream is that we go on trying to get to the cathedral so clearly visible well above us. Later, with the musical *My Fair Lady*, the song that I enjoyed most was the one sung by Stanley Holloway – "Get me to the church, get me to the church on time."

During my short time as Archdeacon of London, I was asked by the bishop to visit a Freudian psychiatrist, whose daughter very much wanted to be married in church. After this request had been happily decided and duly solemnised, I asked the bride's father if he would psychoanalyse me. I told him that the reason was that with my interest in Buddhism I might get some light on the self, and also would be glad to understand myself more deeply. The Harley Street specialist flatly refused, and when I asked him the reason why, he said that in our talks together he had come to the conclusion that I was a man with a lively faith, whereas in treating many clergy the result had been that they had lost their faith. I did venture to suggest that what had really happened was that the consequence of analysis had exposed that they had no faith. He was adamant in his refusal and urged me to go to a Jungian whom he could recommend who would treat the religious factors more seriously.

My interest in dreams continued in Perth, and one Lent I preached a course of mid-week addresses on the dreams of the Bible, including the dreams of Joseph, Jacob and Elijah in the older Testament and those of Joseph of Nazareth, Peter and Paul in the additional Testament. After the first address a lady came to tell me of a dream that she had had on the previous night. She was standing on the edge of a swimming bath with her two small daughters, knowing that there was a crocodile in the bath. She immediately dashed round to the wheel which drained the water away, only to discover that all that was left was just a big lizard. I knew that only the dreamer could interpret his/her own dreams, and explained that I thought of a dream as a sealed envelope with the dreamer's name on it. We went on to discuss what had been in her mind in the day or two preceding the dream. She confided in me that the two daughters were from a previous marriage and she feared that her second husband was having a bad effect on the two little girls. I enquired if she could see any connection between what she felt and the actual dream, to which she replied, "Are you suggesting that what I feared as a crocodile was only a harmless lizard?" I said that only she could decide that question. The next week she came to me to say that she had told the dream and its suggested interpretation to her husband, and that a new relationship had resulted, and the upshot was that the four of them were going on a trip to Japan to initiate a happy future.

Two years later, on the day before I left Perth for Jerusalem, she came to visit me again, saying that she could not let me leave without a further word of thanks to me for helping her discover the meaning of her remarkable dream.

I remember another confidence I received from that lenten course. An elderly woman told me of a nightmare that came to her repeatedly. She was running along a corridor with no doors on either side, pursued by a terrifying unseen animal. There was a closed door at the end of the corridor which she managed to open, only to find herself in the arms of her husband. I found myself asking her if she was afraid of death, to which she indignantly replied that she was a Christian and moreover the widow of a priest. Gentle prompting resulted in her readiness to consider this, but I never heard the outcome.

Let me return to my Freudian friend and his advice to consult a Jungian. In my very busy life I could not find time and opportunity to do so, but I eagerly read and studied Jung's books, and was greatly helped by *Modern Man in Search of a Soul*. Recently there have been some striking television and radio programmes about Jung's thought and work, summarised in a book entitled *The Wisdom of the Dream*. The writers of that book said that Jung was characterised by three things – honesty, humility, and humour, the "three H's" as they called them. Reading Jung's books convinced me of the importance of the subconscious – my own as well as the common subconscious which we share with our fellow-humans. I was particularly interested in his two orientations of introvert and extrovert, in his four types of thinking, intuition, sensation and feeling, and in his explanation that the intuitive type goes by hunches, sees round corners, smells a rat in almost every situation. He said that many bankers, doctors, even gamblers act intuitively. I was rather surprised that he did not include religious ministers, or stress that the intuitive faculty was more common in women than in men. Another point that attracted me was his theory of the shadow, which seemed to me to relate to the teaching of Jesus about seeing the mote in the eye of another, without being aware of the log of wood in my own eye. Jung made me ask myself the question, "What is it that I am seeing in the other person that is mine?" His statement that "The dream presents perhaps the largest number of non-rational factors, such as lack of logic, questionable morality, uncouth form and apparent absurdity or nonsense. Often people dismiss dreams as stupid, meaningless and worthless," helped me considerably in the many times that my own dreams seemed to have these undesirable features, crystallising in the verdict that the unconscious is not subject to our conscious values. He felt and said that our modern European life is such that our time pressures and materialistic attitudes give us little time for our dreams. What I have tried to express in this long paragraph is my debt to Jung in the understanding of my own instinctive life, in my preaching and in my pastoral care for those who still come to me troubled by problems of conscience and relations with others. One surprising insight that has only come to me recently was his comment that Hitchcock with his terrifying stories of horrors was looking at the human condition and was not afraid to show us "the dark stuff".

Another writer whom I never met but who has greatly helped in my search is Teilhard de Chardin, the Jesuit priest and palaeontologist whose writings were forbidden to be published by the Vatican. He had the foresight and determination to write them down, and after his death on Easter Day 1955 his admirers and friends published them in French and they were quickly translated and published in English. His greatest book was thought by many to be *The Phenomenon of Man*, in which he examined man as a phenomenon, without religious and theological assumptions, studying him empirically, historically and scientifically, and then relating his findings to theological interpretation and devotional faith. Julian Huxley in his introduction to it wrote: "In my view he achieved a remarkable success and opened up vast territories of thought to further exploration and mapping."

A thought that thrilled me as I wrestled with this great book was his vision of an "Omega point" towards which everything is converging, a theme which was shared by other thinkers without Teilhard's religious commitment but perceived from their own study of the phenomenal and empirical.

Teilhard made a great leap of faith in identifying this point of convergence with Christ. I later wondered if it would not have been better to identify it with God, the Alpha and Omega of Christian faith, and to think of Christ as the penultimate, leading to the final experience of the spiritual. Teilhard saw six stages of growth as vitalising matter, humanising life, unifying mankind, spiritualising man, Christifying men and incorporating them into the eternal. He laid great stress on Paul's emphasis on the *pleroma*, the plenitude, the fulfilment and consummation of the world in Christ. Creation is not yet finished and eagerly awaits the commitment and co-operation of the children of God (Romans 8:22 and 8:19). "Man can no longer be content with family, country, making money, ambition. He will want wider organisations to create, new paths to blaze, causes to uphold, truths to discover, an ideal to cherish and defend within himself."

This last quotation is from the book of Teilhard that I found most exhilarating, *Le Milieu Divin*, which is a continuous prayer to God. I can quote only one or two sentences which thrilled me. He talks of losing oneself in the depth of God:

To adore . . . That means to lose oneself in the unfathomable, to plunge into the unexhaustible, to find peace in the incorruptible, to be absorbed in defined immensity, to offer

192

oneself to the fire and the transparency, to annihilate oneself in proportion as one becomes more deliberately conscious of oneself, and to give of one's deepest to that whose depth has no end.

A further paragraph to which I return again and again reads:

Every man in the course of his life, must not only show himself obedient and docile. By his fidelity he must *build*, starting with the most natural territory of his own self – a work into which something enters from all the elements of the earth. *He makes his own soul* throughout all his earthly days; and at the same time he collaborates in another work, which infinitely transcends the perspectives of his individual achievement: the completing of the world.

I cannot omit one or two shorter memorable sayings. "Whatever happens is to be adored", for God is in it to bring blessing and enabling graces.

A warning is sounded in the statement, "God created heaven and earth; man has created hell, and each man is responsible for making his own hell."

Finally, in my memory: "Not everything is God, but God is in everything, and everything in God."

And my "amen" comes in a prayer of Teilhard that I could make my own:

O God, grant that at all times You may find me as You desire me, and where You would have me be, that You may lay hold on me fully, both by the Within and the Without of myself, grant that I may never break this double thread of my life.

I believe that Teilhard would have rejoiced in the inspiration of another great scientist, Sir Alister Hardy, the great marine biologist of Oxford, who in addition to his scientific books like

193

The Living Stream founded the Religious Experience Research Unit, which collected the personal accounts of several thousand people, and examined them deeply to discover more of the practice of spirituality. I was fortunate in getting to know Sir Alister intimately in his closing years, and rejoiced in the award to him of the Templeton Prize a short while before he died, the bulk of which he gave to found a research centre for the study of religious experience.

I was fortunate also in somehow getting to know the writings of Helen Waddell, particularly her two volumes of translations of *Mediaeval Latin Lyrics,* the translations being poetry of a very high order in their own right. My desire to learn more about Helen was more than satisfied in the biography written by Dame Felicitas Corrigan, a nun of the well-known Roman Catholic convent Stanbrook Abbey, near Worcester, who edited the second volume of lyrics which Helen had not been able to finish before she died.

I have been thrilled by an insight in the opening four verses of a New Testament book which in most English versions of the Bible is headed "The Second Epistle of Peter", a designation which is questioned by some biblical scholars. I have already quoted from this passage in a different context. The writer, speaking in the apostle's name, greets its readers as those who have been granted "precious and very great promises . . . that you may escape from the corruption that is in the world . . . and become partakers of the divine nature" (2 Pet. 1:4). This has meant to me that God has put something of himself in our human life, a seed of divinity, a miniature transplant of himself which has the potential of what we see perfectly fulfilled in Jesus Christ, whom we may think of as the first perfect Child of God, who exemplified the Eternal in his life, ministry, death and risen life.

Let me finally conclude this chapter of grateful acknowledgement of my debt to the many friends mentioned in this search of mine and in my cross-examination of what I have learnt of myself, with some words of St Paul in his anthem on love contained in the thirteenth chapter of his first epistle to the Christians of Corinth:

> For our knowledge is imperfect and our prophecy is imperfect; but when the perfect comes, the imperfect will pass away . . . Now we see in a mirror *(a metal one)* dimly, but then face to face. Now I know in part; then shall I understand fully, even as I have been fully understood.

CHAPTER 19

God Completing his Universe

As one grows old and becomes aware of one's migration to whatever is ahead, one looks back with gratitude, and inevitably compares the present with what is past. There have been more changes in this twentieth century than in any other previous century of which we have records or about which geologists, archaeologists and anthropologists are discovering for us.

For anyone who like myself has lived all his life in a Christian environment, one can see changes in our idea of God, changes in our thinking about the Bible, changes in social conditions, changes in church attendance. We endeavour to pass some judgement on those changes and trace deepening understanding of meaning and purpose in the whole human tapestry, which can be attributed to the unceasing activity of God.

The basic problem is how to adjust our thinking and behaviour to the amazing development in technology. There is now so much power in the minds of people which can be used for good or evil, for constructive or destructive purposes. Computers help us to calculate in a few minutes things which formerly took months to work out. The one development that impresses me most is a growth in compassion. In natural catastrophes involving widespread suffering nations are quick to make grants to help the nation that is reeling under the blow.

Another surprising reaction is that in dire emergencies the army is sent in to organise the relief available. This suggests an altogether new role for armies. Further, there is growing a standing provision of tents, blankets, tinned foods and medicines which can be immediately drawn upon as the need arises.

Refrigeration makes it possible to store chemicals at the right temperatures for injections to tackle infectious viruses.

It is as if the prophet Micah's vision of beating swords into ploughshares, and spears into pruning hooks, is being fulfilled in an advanced way – bombers are being transformed into mercy planes, and tanks into mechanical ploughs and combine-harvesters, trees are being planted to tackle erosion, spraying from planes destroys clouds of locusts. With these new devices burdensome agricultural labour is relieved.

It is admitted that these new technological processes are expensive, but they cost only a fraction of the expenditure on armaments. It is said that a five per cent reduction in arms expenditure all round would bring about the economic change necessary. One thing that is becoming apparent, both in developed wealthy countries and in poor developing countries, is the need for pure drinking water. The World Health Organisation tells us that two thirds of the world's population does not yet have it.

Ever since my earliest days in the villages of the Irrawaddy Delta I have been interested in meeting this need, and so avoiding the many diseases of the stomach, kidneys and digestive organs. There seem to be great quantities of water imprisoned deep below the earth's surface. There are powerful machines which bore through earth and rock to release vast quantities of water uncontaminated by surface impurities. Artesian wells are sunk by which, once the pipe is driven into the underground water, a stream gushes to the surface with its own spontaneous force.

In the last two to three years I have been fortunate in getting to know two water engineers, father and son, in Cumbria, who have invented a pump to deal with water near the surface, which can be operated by women. To the pump they have attached a filter which is 75 per cent effective in purification; and I am sure that both George and Richard Cansdale are constantly at work to improve this figure. Recently the son went to Zambia to superintend the installation of 150 pumps, train village women to operate them, and investigate the possibility of manufacturing the pumps in that country. The Cansdales are greatly encouraged by a grant from Rotary International for every pump supplied. The cost of each pump works out at £140, covering air freight and installation.

We can thank God that in our century our attitude to war has changed radically. This change has been brought about partly by the tremendous slaughter of two world wars, calculated by some to be not less than 47 million deaths. War is no longer fought between comparatively small professional armies but conscription covers all men of miliary age, and now also the recruitment of women, and the mobilisation of the whole nation on a war footing. The discovery of nuclear energy heightens radically the destructiveness of war, and the very fear of nuclear attack is a deterrent towards its taking place, with the prospect of immediate, almost simultaneous retaliation. It is said by those who study nuclear warfare that human life could become extinct by such an outbreak.

We are told that the United States has nuclear bombs that could destroy everyone in Russia twenty times over. In the same way Russia has bombs which could kill everyone in the USA twenty times over. I thank God that we are being made aware of these warning facts, so that we can ensure that nuclear warfare does not break out. Both warning and saving signs come, I believe, from God, who is always at work for human unity, justice and peace, often in surprising ways.

The Book of Isaiah speaks of God working in new ways to achieve his will for the world:

> Behold, I am doing a new thing;
>   now it springs forth, do you not perceive it?
> I will make a way in the wilderness
>   and rivers in the desert (43:19).

In the first of four passages concerning the Servant of the Lord, the writer or editor says:

> Behold, the former things have come to pass,
>   and new things I now declare;

198

before they spring forth
I tell you of them (42:9).

In the closing chapters, the prophet hears God saying:

Behold, I create new heavens and a new earth;
and the former things shall not be remembered
or come into mind.
But be glad and rejoice for ever
in that which I create;
for behold I create Jerusalem a rejoicing,
and her people a joy . . .
No more shall there be in it
an infant that lives but a few days,
or an old man who does not fill out his days;
for the child shall die a hundred years old,
and the sinner a hundred years old
shall be accursed.
They shall build houses and inhabit them;
they shall plant vineyards and eat their fruit
. . . for like the days of a tree shall the
days of my people be,
and my chosen shall long enjoy the work of their hands.
They shall not labour in vain,
or bear children for calamity . . .

The writer goes on to picture this new world when

The wolf and the lamb shall feed together;
the lion shall eat straw like the ox;
and dust shall be the serpent's food.
They shall not hurt or destroy
in all my holy mountain, says the Lord. (65:17-25)

The passage just quoted is very similar to an earlier extract, which adds the lovely touch of a baby playing happily over the

199

hole of the asp and the weaned infant putting his hand into the adder's nest, and most touching of all, a little child shall lead a procession of the animals following protectively and trustfully (see 11:6-9).

The holy mountain of Jerusalem is a symbol for the whole earth, and the temple a centre to which all nations shall come and pray (56:7).

This lenghty string of Isaianic passages emphasises the new, unexpected, surprising things that God is always doing, and urges us today to look out for the same kind of divine deeds.

Two short sayings from Alcuin, the English head of Charles the Great's palace school, have helped me to crystallise my thinking about war. The first is:

> That road is closed to war, whose gate
> stands open to the stars.

The second speaks of the eternal will to peace:

> One goodness ruleth by its single will
> all things that are, and have been
> and shall be.

I am greatly relieved and thankful for another change during my lifetime, a new attitude to suicide. For years I was bothered by the ruling that suicides should not be buried in consecrated ground nor should the Prayer Book service be used without alteration for the funeral. Finally I decided to ignore such inhuman instructions whenever I conducted the funeral of anyone who had committed suicide, inspired by our Lord's first prayer on the cross and believing that he included poor Judas in his compassion and excusing.

Recently the Mother of the Sisters of the Love of God at Fairacres in Oxford was distressed by the suicide of someone close to her and wrote a prayer on the sad occasion, a copy of which she kindly sent to me. I am grateful for permission given me to include it in this chapter:

> O God Righteous and Compassionate
> Forgive the despair of . . . for whom we pray.
> Heal in him that which is broken
> And in your great Love stand with those
> Hurt by the violence of his end.
> Lord, be to him not a Judge but a Saviour:
> Receive him into that Kingdom wherein by your mercy
> We sinners also would have place
> Through the merits of our Wounded Redeemer
> Who lives and reigns with you in the Holy Spirit's power
> Now and unto the Ages of Ages. Amen.

The New Testament equally emphasises the new and the unexpected and the surprising. God is not only at work throughout his creation, but also in our human experience. Father Gerard Hughes, a Jesuit priest, pictures life as a journey in which we are all engaged, which began with our conception and ends with our death. He feels keenly the confusion, bewilderment or illusion in which people live. But equally he believes that God is the God of surprises, who breaks into our closed minds, self-centredness and fears. God is our treasure, hidden within our own experience, a seed of eternity and divinity sown within us.

St Paul emphasises the great change that comes about in true conversion: "If anyone is in Christ, he is a new creation; the old has passed away, the new has come." Not only is the individual radically changed, but the world also: "God was in Christ, reconciling the world to himself and entrusting to us the message of reconciliation . . ." So we are ambassadors for Christ, God making his appeal through us (2 Cor. 5:17-20).

Far from inflicting suffering on us humans, either as punishment or for our own good, God takes upon Himself the pain of the world. Gerard Hughes castigates the complacency of many of us in the Church and our prayers for the solutions of the

201

world's problems, without for a moment considering that we may be contributing to them. A paragraph that penetrated my heart and mind came from his own experience and enlightened mind:

> I begin to see that the real battle is not in working to change the structure of the Church and of society, but in struggling to change the structure of my own psyche. This may sound very individualistic and selfish, but the only thing we can change is ourselves, for the only power that can bring creative change is God. I cannot domesticate God, I cannot tell him what to do, no matter how noble the cause: all I can do is to let his glory shine through me. Let God be God in my own life.

Father Hughes sees God operating in the minds of many who do not profess to be Christians:

> The majority of mankind may not know or acknowledge the Christian God by name, but they meet Him in their own hearts when they feed the hungry, give drink to the thirsty, shelter the homeless, relieve the suffering, show under- standing, act justly and live with integrity. God weeps and loves in them. They go out to God when they show compassion, they reject Him when they grow callous to human suffering by so concentrating on their own security and well-being that they are willing to risk millions of lives and hold millions in subjection in order to obtain it.

When we see God at work he works surprises:

> We begin to see that our national security is in sharing, not in hoarding, our welfare is in a spirit of co-operation, not ruthless competition, in cherishing nature not in exploiting it, in trying to understand rather than in condemning, in recognising the dignity of each human being rather than in

rating their value by their earning power or their rank in society.

Father Gerard ends his penultimate chapter with the assurance that, thinking and living in the way for which he has pleaded, the surprising thing will be that we shall be able to say with St Paul: "For it is when I am weak that I am strong." (2 Cor.12:10)

The prophet Ezekiel has a vision which is full of surprises. He is in a valley full of bones, very dry, showing that they are the bones of people long dead. In the vision he is asked, "Can these bones live?" He knows that only the power of God can enable them to do so. He is told to pronounce over them the word of the Lord. When he does so there is a great rattling and the bones fit themselves into complete skeletons. Then flesh and sinews come upon them, and skin covers them into complete corpses, but still there is no breath in them. He is then told to speak a further word from the Lord. "Come from the four winds, O breath, and breathe upon these slain that they may live." Again he obeys, the breath comes, the bodies become alive, and get up on their feet, "an exceeding great host."

Then the prophet understands the meaning. The bones are the whole of Israel, who feel completely cut off and hopeless. The nation is to be revived. He hears the divine voice once more: "I will put my Spirit within you and you shall live, and I will place you in your own land; then you shall know that I, the Lord, have spoken, and have fulfilled my promise." The vision brought new hope to the prophet and he was able to bring back hope to the nation with authority and confidence.

John the Apostle, in vision, also sees a new heaven and earth. He is in exile on the Isle of Patmos, cut off from his flock, so he must have felt relieved that there was no more sea. He sees the Holy City, new Jerusalem, coming down out of heaven, sparkling with beauty. A little later he hears a voice saying,

"Look, the dwelling place of God is with men. He will make his home with them and they shall be his people. God will wipe away every tear, and there shall be no more death, and so no more grief and weeping. There shall be no more pain, for all such things are things of the past." A great voice came from the throne, saying, "Behold, I make all things new." (Rev. 21:3-5)

The vision is continued of the Holy City, bright with a heavenly radiance, with a high wall surrounding it, four-square, with twelve gates, representing the twelve tribes, and twelve foundations with the names of the twelve apostles inscribed on them. This partnership of Old and New Testaments, Jews and Christians, shows both continuity and spiritual relationship.

The City has no need of sun and moon, for Christ is its light. The gates of it are always open so that all nations may bring their offerings of worship. The only people who are not allowed to enter it are those judged as unclean by falsehood and abominable practices.

The one feature which might be thought surprising at first sight is that there is no temple in it. The presence of God and Christ with God no longer requires any buildings and other symbols. Perfection has come, no human language can describe its excellence – we shall see God face to face and have the mark of eternity, sanctity and life upon our foreheads. Surrounding the throne will be a crowd which no one can number from all races and languages, joining with angels and saints and with all the company of heaven, singing the same song which Isaiah heard: "Holy, holy, holy Lord, heaven and earth are full of your glory. Glory be to you, O Lord most high."

Looking back with gratitude for the past, and looking forward with hope for the future, we can say with Isaiah the prophet and with St Paul the missioner to the world:

What no eye has seen, nor ear heard,
nor the heart of man conceived,
what God has prepared for those who love Him.

(1 Cor.2:9; Isaiah 64:4)

CHAPTER 20

Towards the Beyond

Many Christians, myself included, often wish that Jesus had lived on to old age, so that he might have given us a model for growing old. He was certainly observant, as in his words to Peter, after the experience of his risen nature by the lake of Galilee: "Truly, truly, I say to you, when you were young you girded yourself (*dressed yourself*) and walked where you would; but when you are old, you will stretch out your hands and another will carry you where you do not wish to go" (John 21:18). The diminishments and irritations of old age, and especially the embarrassment of bladder and bowels, failing eyesight and hearing, together with false teeth, however efficient our dentist may be, are all very trying. When these problems became almost unbearable, I remember a prayer which somewhere I picked up along the last stretch of life. I have adapted it to my own need:

> Dear God and Father, we pray
> as our strength falls away,
> the will may grow firmer,
> the courage braver,
> and the spirit holier,
> as in the company of your beloved Son
> we begin to grow like him,
> and with him come to You,
> the Eternal, the Perfect,
> the never failing Love,
> Blessed and blessing for ever.

Teilhard de Chardin used to speak of being emptied and stripped of unnecessary baggage, filled with the Spirit. He did not live on into the seventies and eighties as many of us do today, but he began to feel the pains and strains of old age.

St Paul in his letter to his dear friends at Philippi, said that he was ready to accept any loss for the sake of Christ:

> I count everything as loss because of the surpassing worth of knowing Christ Jesus my Lord. For his sake I have suffered the loss of all things, and count them as refuse, in order that I may gain Christ and be found in him . . . that I may know him and the power of his resurrection, and may share his sufferings, becoming like him in his death, that if possible I may attain the resurrection from the dead (3:8-11).

He goes on to admit that he has not yet reached this stage or is already perfect, but

> I press on to make it my own, because Christ Jesus has made me his own . . . but one thing I do, forgetting what lies behind and straining forward to what lies ahead, I press on toward the goal for the prize of the upward call of God in Christ Jesus (3:12-14).

This short passage in a favourite epistle needs much more deepening meditation, silently allowing each phrase to make its impression on mind and heart, with a readiness to put into practice any intuition which we believe comes from God.

In the second epistle to Timothy, whoever may have been the actual writer, a moving reminiscence of St Paul is included as he surveys his whole life, expecting that he will have to suffer a painful death in the near future:

> I am already on the point of being sacrificed; the time of my departure has come. I have fought the good fight, I have finished the race, I have kept the faith. Henceforth there is

206

laid up for me the crown of righteousness, which the Lord, the righteous judge will award to me on that Day, and not only to me but also to all who have loved his appearing (2 Tim. 4:6-8).

I hope that when the time of my departure comes, I shall be able to echo the same.

St Paul gives us further insights into the meaning of death:

This perishable nature must put on the imperishable, and this mortal nature must put on immortality. When the perishable puts on the imperishable, and the mortal puts on immortality, then shall come to pass the saying that is written:

"Death is swallowed up in victory."
"O death, where is thy victory?
O death, where is thy sting?"

He then makes his own thanksgiving:

Thanks be to God, who gives us the victory through our Lord Jesus Christ. Therefore, my beloved brethren, be steadfast, immovable, always abounding in the work of the Lord, knowing that in the Lord your labour is not in vain. (1 Cor. 15:53-8)

Yet with all Paul's words of comfort many of us are afraid of death, physical death. In the historical books of the Older Testament, it is said of many of the kings of Israel and Judah, that they slept with their fathers, and the day of death was spoken of as the time when they would be with the fathers. May we not see in such mention an implicit faith in life after death which would be something far above the then popular idea of a shadowy existence much less than physical life.

David, weeping over Bathsheba's child, paradoxically

mourned: "I shall go to him, but he shall not return to me" (2 Sam 12:23). In the New Testament death is spoken of as "falling asleep," but the sense I find here is that death is as easy as falling asleep here and waking up there in a new form of existence. St John comes to the rescue of struggling faith with his assurance that "There is no fear in love, but perfect love casts out fear" (1 John 4:18). I recognise that John's words refer primarily to God's love for us, but they quickly become relevant to our love for him.

Both Testaments speak of all of us being sojourners in this life, only here for a short time, as the author of Psalm 39 says: "For I am a stranger with thee, and a sojourner as all my fathers were." We are only here on the earth for a short time (so it seems to those of us in old age). Our permanent home is elsewhere, as the author of the epistle to the Hebrews says of the men of faith who acknowledged that they were strangers and exiles seeking a homeland, "looking forward to the city which has foundations, whose builder and maker is God." In a later verse he says that God has prepared for them *(such)* a city (Heb. 11:10, 13-16).

St Peter, in his first epistle, says that we who believe in Christ have been born again to a living hope through the resurrection of Jesus Christ from the dead, which guarantees to us an inheritance which is imperishable, undefiled, and unfading . . . for a salvation ready to be revealed in the *(our?)* last time (1 Peter 1:3-5).

I sometimes wonder how all this is relevant to those who die in violence and terrorism, or who would die in a nuclear war. Christ again comes to our aid in Luke 12:4-5.

> I tell you, my friends, do not fear those who kill the body, and after that have no more that they can do. But I will warn you whom to fear: fear him who, after he has killed, has power to cast into hell.

My own personal interpretation is that it is not God who will kill the soul and cast it into hell. For he is the soul's Creator and Saviour. He does not create hell. We make our own hell, but are free to escape from it at any time by accepting his saving love and grace.

In addition to the physical accompaniments of old age, there is a mental and spiritual factor which I had noticed with older friends whom I had admired, but in my mind felt rather critical about. This was the depression which characterised almost every one of them. I had not then realised that it came with old age. It certainly came to me, but only occasionally could I identify a blameworthy cause. Yet I felt generally depressed. Finally I came to think of it as a temptation that needed to be resisted, and by the help of God and his Risen Christ overcome. The feeling still persisted, but now I felt a strange comfort, that most, if not all old people suffered from it. A further difficulty lay in remembering immediately that God's grace was in the temptation, not that it was caused by him, nor was it his will, but his opportunity to come to the rescue. It is also a help to *do* something practical rather than sit and mope self-pityingly. We need to adjust ourselves to the new situation, especially if we had been in a position of having to make decisions as part of the job we had accepted.

It is not an easy thing to accept that one is on the shelf, more a spectator than a participator. In this struggle I was unexpectedly helped by learning from friends in Beersheba University that their agricultural researchers had produced a strain of tomato that would last three months on the shelf!

A pleasing surprise of old age is the joy in grandchildren. The birth of a grandchild recalls the happiness experienced in the birth of the mother or father. There is also the joy in knowing that the family will be continued. Grandparents have more unhurried time to spend with grandchildren, for the parents are preoccupied in making a livelihood or providing a comfortable, happy home. Also the grandparents usually have some savings, which enable them to give an occasional present on which the youngest may have set their heart.

Each Christian has to relate his own experience and hope to the insights of the men and women of faith in the Bible. When I retired from Jerusalem at the age of seventy-two, my wife's health was failing and we had no settled home to which we could retire. We were fortunate in being able to find a derelict cottage in a hamlet near Wantage, which a local architect and builder very skilfully reconstructed into an attractive house, which my wife eagerly gave her energies into making a gracious and comfortable home, as she had for some years back been longing to do. We worked hard in house and garden, until one evening she collapsed. Our doctor came at once and diagnosed a severe stroke and warned my daughter and myself that she would die within the next day or so. Margaret and I felt that she would certainly do so if we let her be taken to hospital. It was a miracle that she did not, and on later visits the doctor always addressed her as the woman who ought to have died.

Loving and nursing care helped her towards partial recovery, but she couldn't talk, and could only walk a few uncertain steps. She never wept or showed a complaining attitude. In a few months we were able to take her to our village church to Evensong. And there we discovered that she could sing, and I can see her now, holding on to the pew in front of her and joining in the sung part of the service. So every morning when bringing her an early cup of tea we would sing, "Good morning to you, good morning, dear Marjorie, good morning to you!" to the tune of the birthday greeting which we had previously sung to the children. She always joined in readily and happily.

As she improved, my wife was able to sit in the garden under a shady tree and look at picture books, especially those of countries where we had lived and worked together. She always wanted to listen to the BBC nine o'clock news, and on occasions when I happened to be reading or playing patience, would somehow attract my attention and point to the clock with her active hand. She could tell the time but she couldn't speak it.

After a few months, the Australian priest who had been my very able chaplain in Perth and Jerusalem, Maurice Coombs, invited me to take a week's mission in his well-to-do parish church in Philadephia. The travelling expenses and honorarium were generous enough to pay tourist excursion fares for my wife, daughter and myself. So all three of us went, plus a very effective folding wheelchair. Visits to the toilet were a problem, but stewards male and female were most helpful, and Maurice and Mary Coombs were waiting for us at John F. Kennedy Airport, and we were soon on the fast turnpike roads to Philadephia.

The exciting moment at The Oak Road Rectory each day was getting the wheelchair and its precious occupant up and down the staircase. Fortunately it was a wide one, and with four able adults, two female and two male, the morning and evening episode was safely and often hilariously managed.

We spent ten days in Philadelphia, and a further ten days in the home of Peggy and Etienne Boegner, the generous creator of the Garden of Prayer in Jerusalem. The flight back to London was a night plane, which was much easier for the heroine of the adventure than the day flight on which we had come.

Gradually my wife needed more expert care than we could get in the hamlet near Wantage, so we had to sell the cottage and move into Oxford, where I was able to rent a flat in a nursing home, and also act as chaplain. The great unexpected mercy was that in a flat next door there lived a retired disabled nurse who became a devoted carer for the two of us. Without Sister Monica Evans we could not possibly have managed. With her presence I was able to make one or two visits to the Middle East, and she would make a big calendar of the days I would be away and mark off each day at a time, and so keep my wife happy and hopeful.

In 1979 we celebrated our golden wedding, with a large party of relatives and friends, and I was happy to note that my wife could recognise everyone present and look up with a smile at me when our joint health was proposed. I think that was the point which she had set her heart on reaching, for soon after, her condition deteriorated. On Easter Sunday 1980 I took her in her wheelchair round some of the roads in North Oxford, and we admired some of the early flowering shrubs and trees. I think she probably had another stroke, and soon she became seriously ill.

211

On the Wednesday in the second week after Easter, she was unconscious, but I sang the daily morning greeting to her and saw that her lips moved to join in. My heart leapt up in the hope that a miracle was taking place, but that same afternoon she died, and the doctor led our two daughters and me into the sitting room, so that the body might be cared for. That night I found it difficult to get to sleep and so read some of our favourite poems, including the one from Elizabeth Barrett Browning which opens with the question, "How do I love thee?" and ends with the lines

> . . . I love thee with the breath,
> Smiles, tears, of all my life. And if God choose,
> I shall but love thee better after death.

That last line has been fulfilled. Every night before going to sleep I try to tell her of the happenings of the past day, good and not so good. I know that before long I shall make my final migration, and join her.

As I look forward to reunion with loved ones and friends who have entered the beyond already, my closing words are a prayer written by Eric Milner-White:

> Withhold not from me, O my God, the best,
>   the spirit of thy dear Son:
> that in that day when the judgement is set
>   I may be presented unto thee
>   not blameless but forgiven,
>   not effectual but faithful,
>   not holy but persevering,
>   without desert but accepted,
> because he hath pleaded the causes of my soul,
>   and redeemed my life.